Roy

COOK
BOOK

Produced by the Publishing Division
of The Automobile Association

Copy editor: Gail Harada

Consultant cookery editor: Catherine Wraight

Illustrator: Peter Neame

Typeset by: Butler & Tanner Ltd, Frome, Somerset
Printed and bound by: Scotprint Ltd, Musselburgh, Scotland

© The Royal National Lifeboat Institution 1989

A CIP catalogue record of this book is available from
the British Library

ISBN 0 86145 883 4

Published for the RNLI by The Automobile Association, Fanum House,
Basingstoke, Hampshire RG21 2EA

FOREWORD

The RNLI is a totally voluntary organisation and depends enormously on the support received from its 2,000 branches and guilds throughout the UK and Republic of Ireland. From flag days, coffee mornings and a wide range of other fund raising activities organized by branch and guild members, comes a substantial part of the RNLI's annual income.

Mr and Mrs Michael Pooley, members of the Pinner (Middlesex) branch, have demonstrated just how enthusiastic and successful is the support of our voluntary workers by their diligent efforts in helping to produce this superb cook book. Originally, their idea had been to produce a modest booklet of recipes collected from local celebrities to help boost branch funds. However, so infectious was their enthusiasm that recipes came flooding in from well over 180 well-known celebrities – far too many for a simple booklet printed in-house! Undaunted, their next task was to find a sponsor, and thanks to The Automobile Association, this too was soon achieved.

Like all lifeboat activities, this new and exciting cook book has been a matter of teamwork. Our lifeboat crews work as a team to carry out their successful rescues. They are supported by a team of staff dedicated to providing the best boats and equipment available. These efforts are only made possible by the team efforts of our fund raisers. The cook book deserves to sell well and I am certain that it will be a huge success, given all the goodwill that has gone into it. My thanks go to Mr and Mrs Pooley, the AA and, last but not least, the many celebrities who gave their time and support in sending their favourite recipes.

Bon appetit!

Lieutenant Commander Brian Miles, RD, RNR Director of the RNLI

INTRODUCTION

This book, as well as giving an insight into what food the stars enjoy, is also a very practical and useful aid to cooking, and will appeal to cooks of all abilities.

It consists of the favourite recipes of about 150 celebrities, many of whom have added comments about their choice, or the kind of food they like, arranged alphabetically within courses.

There are also recipes from four lifeboat crews, and these can be found throughout the book separating the courses, which range from soups, suppers and main courses, to a selection of the more unusual in the miscellaneous section.

Join the regulars of the Rover's Return in *Coronation Street* for a plate of Betty's famous Traditional Lancashire Hotpot. Discover how to prepare Roy Castle's Stuffed Camel, or for more discerning tastes, try Sir Ralph Halpern's Chicken Stuffed with Asparagus and Lime Mousse, followed by Maurice Colbourne's Cardamom Ice Cream.

All the contributions come complete with both imperial and metric measurements and are accompanied by either a photograph of the contributor or a specially drawn illustration.

So many celebrities have responded to the invitation from the RNLI and the AA to contribute to this book that it has not been possible to include them all, and special thanks are due not only to those whose recipes have been published, but also to the generous people whose names are listed in the acknowledgements on page 160.

CONTRIBUTORS

THE RECIPES

... For Those in Peril on the Sea

Lifeboat call-outs come at all times of the day or night — including meal times. Breakfast, dinner, tea and supper, not to mention weddings, birthdays and Christmas dinners may be interrupted by a MAYDAY call. Lifeboatmen and women are used to reacting immediately and selflessly whenever they receive a distress call and their work increases each year. Although little of this is reported in the media these days, lifeboats are called out at least 10 times every day on average and save at least three lives each day.

Some rescues are long and arduous. A search up to 30 miles out to sea or standing by a disabled cargo ship in storm conditions can last for nine hours or more with only packet soups, hot drinks or chocolate bars to sustain crew and survivors. Other rescues, close to shore, are soon completed. Speed is of the essence when

'RNLB Spirit of Lowestoft'. Lowestoft's lifeboat tows a casualty to safety in rough seas.

Survivors about to board the Weymouth lifeboat.

yachts or dinghies capsize or a child is being swept out to sea on an airbed. By no means are all rescues so dramatic, but when a coxswain and his crew respond to an SOS, their skill and training has prepared them for any situation they might face. Here are some random examples of their work — in each case winning awards of bravery for the lifeboatmen on board.

The crew on Lowestoft's Tyne-class lifeboat were called from their beds just after midnight on a stormy October night. A stricken coaster, *Medina D*, had sent out a MAYDAY call. The boat was holed, listing and bumping the sea bed and her master wanted the crew taken off as soon as possible. The lifeboat launched in pouring rain and battled through a gale force 8

wind in poor visibility until Coxswain John Catchpole found the stricken *Medina D* in the lifeboat's searchlight. He set about evacuating the master and crew from the coaster's port side, but was driven back by steep waves. At the second attempt, two survivors scrambled down the rope ladder to safety. Then a fierce gust threw the lifeboat and the coaster together hurling a seaman on to the deck of the lifeboat, luckily without serious injury. Again, the coxswain skilfully manoeuvred the lifeboat alongside, and as the angry sea drove the two boats together again, a fourth crew member and the master were pulled safely aboard. Within minutes, *Medina D* sank, but the survivors were safely landed back at Lowestoft at 2 am.

Helmsman Alan Clarke and the crew of Hunstanton's Atlantic 21 lifeboat, *Spirit of America*, faced snow, gales and unpenetrable darkness when they answered a MAYDAY call on a February evening. A fishing boat, *Portunus*, disabled by trawl nets round her propeller, was being towed to harbour by tug. However, a badly injured man on board needed urgent medical treatment. The lifeboat raced to the rescue, tossed by 12-ft waves and buffeted by biting winds. It took all of Helmsman Clarke's

An Atlantic 21 class lifeboat in heavy seas.

Rescue is at hand for this fishing boat.

concentration and skill to drive the lifeboat close enough to take the injured man off the fishing boat. The first attempt failed but, on the second, the man was safely transferred to the lifeboat. In atrocious conditions, the lifeboat was driven carefully to shore where an ambulance was waiting to take the injured man to hospital.

Kirkwall's Arun-class lifeboat, *Mickie Salvesen*, launched soon after seven o'clock on a stormy September morning, when the bulk cement-carrier, *BC Mercurius*, had engine trouble and was drifting steadily towards shore. With lashing rain limiting visibility, the lifeboat plunged through heavy seas to her aid. A helicopter had lifted off four crew, but the master and chief engineer remained, hoping to save the ship.

The lifeboat reached the scene at nine o'clock to find the 160-ft ship rolling dangerously with 20-ft waves crashing across her deck. Slowly, and with great precision, Coxswain Sinclair brought the lifeboat alongside, ready to take off the men if needed. A towline was passed to the carrier.

It was slow, painstaking work; gradually the carrier was turned round and prevented from going aground. Twice the line parted as the boats were tossed violently in the storm. Each time, with great difficulty, it was retrieved and re-passed. As the two boats moved away from the shore and conditions eased slightly, the carrier was able to drop anchor. The lifeboat stood by for over two hours until a tug arrived to tow the ship back to Kirkwall. The lifeboat finally arrived back at Kirkwall at nine in the evening — more than 13 hours on duty in atrocious weather and seas.

JOSS
ACKLAND

"Sitting outside on a hot Sicilian evening, drinking cool white wine and eating this delicious pasta, is something to remember."

Pasta with Olives

RECIPE

14 oz (400 g) spaghetti
6 tbs (90 ml) olive oil (preferably green virgin oil)
2 cloves garlic (peeled and crushed)
8 oz (225 g) tomatoes (peeled and chopped)
3 anchovies (finely chopped)
4 green olives (stoned and sliced)
8 black olives (stoned and sliced)
1 tbs (15 ml) capers
salt and pepper

METHOD

Cook the spaghetti in boiling salted water for 10–15 minutes or until cooked. Drain thoroughly.

Heat the oil in a saucepan, add the garlic and cook for 2 minutes. Stir in remaining ingredients and heat through for a minute. Add to the spaghetti and mix well. Serve immediately. *Serves 4.*

Toasted Cheese

RECIPE

2 oz (50 g) butter
1 tsp (5 ml) mustard powder
4 tbs (60 ml) brown ale
8 oz (225 g) mature Cheddar cheese (grated)
salt and freshly ground black pepper
pinch cayenne pepper
8 thick slices bread

METHOD

Melt the butter in a saucepan and add the mustard, brown ale, Cheddar cheese, salt and pepper. Stir continuously over a low heat, until the cheese has melted, but do not allow to boil.

Toast the bread on both sides and spread the cheese mixture over. Sprinkle with a little cayenne pepper (take care, it's very hot) and grill until golden-brown and bubbling. Serve immediately. *Serves 4.*

DAVID BELLAMY

David's wife says the first thing he asks for when he gets home after one of his trips abroad is cheese on toast.

TONY **B**LACKBURN

Tony is a vegetarian and hasn't eaten meat for a number of years. However, this super creamy vegetable soup will go down well with meat-eaters too.

Cream of Vegetable Soup

RECIPE

1 lb (450 g) mixed vegetables (carrots, celery, leeks, cabbage)
2 oz (50 g) butter
1 pt (600 ml) béchamel sauce
½ pt (300 ml) milk
¼ pt (150 ml) cream

METHOD

Peel or scrape and wash the vegetables before chopping finely. Blanch them for 2 minutes in boiling water then drain. Melt the butter in a heavy-based pan over a low heat and cook the vegetables, covered, for 5–6 minutes until soft. Stir in the béchamel sauce and simmer gently for 5 minutes. Rub the mixture through a sieve or liquidise to make a smooth purée. Re-heat the soup, without boiling, over a low heat, thinning with milk if desired. Correct the seasoning and stir in the cream just after serving.

All American Clam Chowder

RECIPE

3 rashers bacon
1 onion (peeled and finely chopped)
7 oz (200 g) can clams (chop, and save liquor)
8 oz (225 g) potatoes (peeled and cubed)
15 oz (425 g) can cream of celery soup
¾ pt (450 ml) milk
dash of pepper

METHOD

Cook the bacon in a frying pan until crisp. Remove and break into 1 in (2.5 cm) pieces. Brown the onion in bacon fat. Add the clam liquor and potatoes. Cover and cook over a low heat until the potatoes are done (about 10 minutes). Stir in half the bacon pieces, chopped clams, and other ingredients. Heat, but do not boil. Garnish the soup with the remaining bacon. *Serves 4.*

ROALD DAHL

"If made in this way, this soup has the most wonderful mushroomy taste. Don't ask me why!"

Mushroom Soup

RECIPE

2 oz (50 g) butter
1 medium onion (chopped)
1 lb (450 g) flat black mushrooms (chopped)
3 tbs (45 ml) fresh parsley (chopped)
1 small crushed garlic clove (optional)
1 ¾ pt (1 l) good chicken stock or substitute some of this with milk if a creamy soup is desired
¼ pt (150 ml) single cream
sprinkle of oregano and marjoram
pinch of ground nutmeg or mace
salt, black pepper (freshly ground)
few drops of Tabasco

METHOD

Melt the butter in a saucepan. Add the onion, garlic (if using), and mushrooms. Cook gently for 5 minutes or until soft. Add 2 tbs (30 ml) of the parsley, the stock (and milk if desired), Tabasco, herbs, nutmeg or mace, and salt and pepper to taste. Bring to the boil, cover and simmer for 10 minutes. Liquidise the soup, then return to the saucepan, add the remaining chopped parsley and cream, and re-heat, but do not boil. Adjust the seasoning if necessary. *Serves 4.*

Eel Soup

RECIPE

8 oz (225 g) potatoes (peeled and diced)
2 oz (50 g) butter
1 oz (25 g) plain flour
½ pt (300 ml) milk
2 tbs (30 ml) chopped parsley
2 tsp (10 ml) capers (chopped)
1 lb (450 g) rock eel (boiled)
non-condiment vinegar
salt and pepper

METHOD

Cook the potatoes in boiling, lightly-salted water for 15 minutes or until cooked. Drain, reserving ½ pt (300 ml) of the cooking liquor. Mash the potatoes with 1 oz (25 g) of the butter.

Melt the remaining butter in a saucepan. Stir in the flour, then gradually add the milk, stirring all the time until the sauce thickens. Simmer for 1 minute. Stir in the parsley and capers then beat into the mashed potato a little at a time. Stir in the reserved cooking liquor. Skin and chop the eel and stir in. Serve hot, sprinkled with vinegar, salt and pepper.

PETER DEAN

Pete Beale from *Eastenders*

KENNY EVERETT

"If your child refuses to eat greens there are two alternatives: don't give him any and watch all his teeth drop out, or feed the little dear with this."

Sprout Soup

RECIPE

1 lb (450 g) Brussels sprouts
1 pt (600 ml) chicken stock
¼ pt (150 ml) milk
½ oz (10 g) cornflour (if necessary)
1 oz (25 g) butter
salt and pepper

METHOD

Take off the outer leaves of the sprouts and make a cross with a knife on each stalk. Put the sprouts in a saucepan with boiling stock. Cook until tender. Put the stock and sprouts into a liquidiser and purée – if you have no liquidiser, press through a fine sieve. Return to the pan, add the milk and season to taste. (This soup is lovely with lots of pepper.) If you like your soup thick, it is at this point you add the cornflour, made to a runny paste with a little milk. At the last moment of cooking stir in the butter. Serve at once. *Serves 4.*

Triple Decker Alph Alpha Toasted Sandwich

RECIPE

3 slices brown bread (toasted)
2 tbs (30 ml) mayonnaise
1 tomato (sliced)
6 thin slices cucumber
2 lettuce leaves (shredded)
½ carton alph alpha (alfalfa) sprouts
½ ripe avocado (peeled and sliced)
salt and pepper

METHOD

Spread one side of each piece of bread with mayonnaise. Mix salad ingredients together and season. Spoon half the salad filling on first slice of toast, top with second slice and remaining salad filling. Finish with third slice of toast.

GORDON THE GOPHER

JAN HARVEY

Lazy Summer Soup

RECIPE

15 oz (425 g) can celery soup (not condensed)
15 fl oz (450 ml) tomato juice
4 oz (100 g) prawns
juice ½ lemon
pinch cayenne pepper
salt and black pepper
4 tbs (60 ml) single cream

METHOD

Whisk soup, juice and cayenne pepper together. Add prawns, lemon juice and season to taste. Chill. Before serving add a swirl of single cream. *Serves 4.*

Peanut Soup

RECIPE

2 oz (50 g) butter
1 large onion (peeled and chopped)
4 sticks celery (washed and finely sliced)
1 oz (25 g) flour
1½ pt (900 ml) vegetable or chicken stock
4 oz (100 g) smooth peanut butter
¼ pt (150 ml) milk or single cream
½ oz (10 g) salted peanuts (chopped)

METHOD

Melt the butter in a saucepan. Add the onion and celery and cook until the onion is soft. Stir in the flour, then gradually add the stock, stirring all the time. Bring to the boil and cook until soft. Add the peanut butter and blend in a blender. Return the purée to the pan, add the milk or cream and reheat, but *do not* boil. Serve with peanuts sprinkled on top. To freeze – do not add the milk or cream. To use, partially thaw, then add milk or cream and heat as above. Freezes for up to 1 month.

NIGEL
HAWTHORNE

DENIS HEALEY

Carrot & Orange Soup

RECIPE

2 medium onions
12 oz (350 g) carrots
1½ oz (30 g) butter
1½ pt (900 ml) chicken or vegetable stock
2 large oranges
1 bay leaf
salt and pepper

METHOD

Roughly chop the onions and carrots. Melt the butter in a saucepan, add the onions and carrots and sauté gently for 5–6 minutes or until soft. Add the stock, the finely grated rind of 1 orange, bay leaf, salt and pepper. Bring to the boil, cover and simmer for 10 minutes.

Rub the mixture through a sieve or liquidise to make a smooth purée. Squeeze the juice from the oranges, add to the purée and reheat. Remove the bay leaf before serving.

This soup is also delicious served chilled in the summer. *Serves 4.*

Sausage & Tomato Pie

RECIPE

1 small onion
2 oz (50 g) butter
1 lb (450 g) pork sausages
2 large tomatoes (peeled and sliced)
salt and pepper
½ pt (300 ml) stock
1 lb (450 g) cooked, mashed potatoes

METHOD

Peel, slice and fry the onion in 1 oz (25 g) of the butter. Grill or fry the sausages, then skin, cut in half lengthways and lay half of them in a pie dish. Cover with the onion and the tomato slices. Add salt and pepper, then place the remaining sausages on top. Pour over the stock, then cover with a thick layer of potatoes. Smooth with a knife then decorate with fork markings. Dot the top with the remaining butter and brown under the grill or bake at Gas Mark 6 or 400°F/200°C for 25 minutes. *Serves 4.*

ROY
HUDD

GLORIA HUNNIFORD

Basic Supper Sauce

RECIPE

$\frac{1}{2}$ oz (10 g) butter
1 large onion (peeled and chopped)
1 lb (450 g) mushrooms (wiped and sliced)
$\frac{1}{2}$ pt (300 ml) milk
dash tomato ketchup
1 tbs (15 ml) sherry
15 oz (425 g) tin condensed mushroom soup
pinch garlic salt
freshly ground black pepper

METHOD

Melt the butter and fry the onion and mushrooms gently until soft. Add the milk and heat through. Stir in the ketchup, sherry, soup and seasonings and mix thoroughly. This forms the basic sauce to which you can add diced cooked chicken, prawns or other seafood. The sauce can be kept warm in the oven until needed. Serve with boiled rice or creamed potato. *Serves 4.*

Pasta Carbonara

RECIPE

1 lb (450 g) spaghetti
3 eggs
2 oz (50 g) grated Parmesan cheese
4 tbs (60 ml) single cream
2 tbs (30 ml) chopped parsley
salt and pepper
½ clove garlic crushed (optional)
2 oz (50 g) butter
8 oz (225g) green bacon [fried or grilled and chopped
into ½ in (1.2 cm) pieces]

METHOD

Cook the spaghetti in plenty of boiling salted water. Drain and keep warm.

Beat together the eggs, cheese, cream, parsley, salt and pepper, and garlic if using. Melt the butter in a large saucepan, add the egg mixture and stir. When the mixture starts to go creamy add the spaghetti and bacon, mix well and serve immediately. *Serves 4.*

JAYNE
IRVING

RUTH
MADOC

"Being Welsh I am very partial to leeks and love to make leek and potato soup. I was recently given a recipe for a quick leek and tomato soup which I find easy and quick to make in the short time I have at home."

Quick Leek & Tomato Soup

RECIPE

1 tbs (15 ml) oil
1 onion (peeled and chopped)
1 garlic clove (peeled and crushed)
1 lb (450 g) leeks (cleaned and chopped)
14 oz (400 g) tin tomatoes
salt and pepper
½ pt (300 ml) beef stock
2 sticks celery (wiped)

METHOD

Fry the onion in oil until soft but not brown. Add the crushed garlic clove and leeks. Fry gently for about 10 minutes, then add the tinned tomatoes, salt, pepper and stock. Cut the celery into small pieces and add. Simmer for a further 10 minutes. Liquidize the mixture, then return to the pan and reheat. Serve with granary rolls. *Serves 4.*

Green Pea Soup

RECIPE

1 oz (25 g) margarine
1 lb (450 g) green split peas
1 large onion (peeled and chopped)
¼ head of celery (including leaves, cleaned and chopped)
2 tomatoes (peeled and chopped)
2 leeks (cleaned and chopped)
salt and pepper

METHOD

Melt the margarine in a large saucepan. Add the onion, celery and leeks and fry lightly for about 8 minutes, or until soft. Add the peas and tomatoes. Cover with water so the vegetables are submerged by 2 in (5 cm). Bring to the boil, cover and simmer gently until everything is soft. Purée in a food processer or mash with a potato masher. Add salt and pepper to taste. Reheat and serve hot.

PAUL & LINDA
McCARTNEY

FRANK
MUIR

The Perfect Lunch
For Elderly Authors

Take one slice of bread from a new loaf not more than three hours old. Place in electric toaster and activate switch. Turn the slice of bread every 20 seconds. First upside down, then back to front, then switch places with the slices and repeat. Wear gloves if fingers begin to blister. When the toast is golden brown, the colour of a good potato crisp, remove and butter moderately. Use a country butter, slightly salted, at blood heat, and butter smoothly right up to the edges of the crusts.

Take a block of fresh, mild, Cheddar cheese, preferably from the West Country, but some East Anglian cheeses are tolerable in an emergency. Carefully slice the pieces exactly $\frac{3}{16}$-inch thick. Make a trial slice first and test thickness with calipers. Assemble the slices of cheese on the buttered surface of the toast in such a manner that the surface is exactly covered. In no circumstances must the cheese protrude beyond the perimeters of the toast. Use a sharp knife to trim off any surplus, working widdershins, *ie*, in an anti-clockwise direction. Nor should gaps be left so that buttered toast is visible between the interstices of the pieces of cheese. Tweezers can be helpful in easing small wedges of cheese into the chinks. Carefully spread on top of the cheese $\frac{1}{2}$ tbs of marmalade. Home-made, of course, and rough cut. Try to obtain navel oranges grown on the hill area 8 miles north of Cadiz; the zest has a fluted aftertaste which compliments the confident, almost jaunty, flavour of the juice. Eat.

Who says that a man cannot make himself a simple meal?

Macaroni Bake

RECIPE

6 oz (175 g) short cut macaroni
2 oz (50 g) English butter
1 onion (peeled and chopped)
12 oz (350 g) minced beef
6 oz (175 g) tin tomatoes
tomato purée to taste

salt and pepper
½ tsp (2.5 ml) dried mixed herbs
1 oz (25 g) plain flour
¾ pt (450 ml) milk
6 oz (175 g) Red Leicester cheese (grated)
1 oz (25 g) peanuts (chopped)

METHOD

Cook the macaroni according to the instructions on the packet; drain well and toss in ½ oz (10 g) of the butter. Melt another ½ oz (10 g) of butter and fry the onion and beef, stirring occasionally, until the meat has browned. Add the tomatoes, purée, seasoning to taste, and herbs. Simmer gently for 10 minutes. Place half the macaroni in an oven-proof dish, cover with the meat mixture, then the remaining macaroni. Place the remaining butter and flour in a saucepan. Mix together, add the milk and heat, stirring continuously until the sauce thickens. Add seasoning and 4 oz (100 g) of the cheese. Pour over the macaroni.

Sprinkle the remaining cheese and peanuts on top. Bake at Gas Mark 6 or 400°F/200°C for 20 minutes. Serve with salad. *Serves 4.*

Consommé Pettifer

RECIPE

15 oz (425 g) tin beef consommé
¼ pt (150 ml) double cream
2 oz (50 g) mock caviar
1 lemon

METHOD

Divide the consommé between 4 bowls and chill for 30 minutes. Whip the double cream. Put one dollop on each bowl of chilled consommé. Sprinkle the mock caviar over the cream. Hang a slice of fresh lemon on the rim of each bowl. *Serves 4.*

"This recipe was given to me by Julian Pettifer."

Kohl Rabi Gratin

RECIPE

2 or 3 large kohl rabi
4 oz (100 g) ham (chopped)
1½ pt (900 ml) cheese sauce
2 oz (50 g) brown breadcrumbs
1 oz (25 g) Cheddar cheese (grated)
1 tomato (sliced)
1 tbs (15 ml) fresh parsley (chopped)

METHOD

Parboil the kohl rabi whole, remove the skins and slice thinly. Arrange in layers in a buttered dish, with chopped ham in between the layers. Alternate the layers with a rich cheese sauce. Finish with a sauce layer, and sprinkle the top with brown breadcrumbs mixed with grated cheese, garnish with tomato slices, sprinkle with parsley and bake in a moderately hot oven at Gas Mark 6 or 400°F/200°C for about 30 minutes. *Serves 6.*

CLAIRE RAYNER

"This is a very suppery dish. It works just as well with celeriacs, turnips or potatoes. I always add onions when I make it with potatoes, though."

CLIFF RICHARD

Cliff tends to eat one main meal a day. He has tea and toast for breakfast, but then tries to avoid eating until the evening. Over the years he has proved this to be the best eating programme in order to keep his weight down and his fitness at peak level for his busy lifestyle and energetic concert performances.

Leek & Potato Soup

RECIPE

1 lb (450 g) potatoes
2 onions
8 oz (225 g) leeks
2 oz (50 g) butter
2 pt (1200 ml) chicken stock
½ tsp (2.5 ml) dried mixed herbs
salt and pepper
¼ pt (150 ml) natural yoghurt

METHOD

Peel the potatoes and cut into small chunks. Chop the onions roughly. Trim the roots and outer leaves from the leeks and wash thoroughly in cold water, then cut into slices.

Melt the butter in a large pan and sauté the potatoes and onions for 5–6 minutes. Add the leeks, stock, herbs, salt and pepper. Simmer for 20 minutes or until the potatoes are cooked. Allow to cool for 10 minutes.

Mix in the yoghurt, then put the soup through a blender at maximum speed.

Serve hot or chill for 2–3 hours and serve cold. *Serves 6.*

Spinach Soup

RECIPE

¾ pt (450 ml) milk
1 onion (peeled)
2 whole cloves
1 bay leaf
1 oz (25 g) butter
1 oz (25 g) plain flour

1 pt (600 ml) chicken stock
salt and pepper
pinch ground nutmeg
1 lb (450 g) fresh spinach
2 tbs (30 ml) double cream (optional)

METHOD

Place the milk in a saucepan with the bay leaf and the onion stuck with cloves. Slowly bring to the boil, remove from the heat and leave to infuse for 20 minutes.

Wash the spinach in plenty of cold water and remove the tough centre rib. Melt ½ oz (10 g) of the butter and sauté the spinach for 10 minutes, or until soft.

Melt the remaining butter, stir in the flour and cook for a minute. Strain the milk and gradually add to the flour mixture. Bring to the boil and simmer for 1 minute. Add to the cooked spinach, then purée in a blender.

Return to the heat and stir in the chicken stock. Season with salt, pepper and nutmeg and reheat gently. Stir in the double cream, if liked. *Serves 4.*

IAN WALLACE

"When I was young I hated soup. However, in my 60s, my wife is constantly having to add to the stock-pot to satisfy my insatiable appetite for the stuff; and it's not because I've lost my teeth, I can gnash a piece of steak with the best of them. A neighbour grows celeriacs and he left one on the doorstep and shoved a copy of his wife's recipe through the letterbox. They're like that in Norfolk."

Celeriac Soup with Dill

RECIPE

8 oz (225 g) celeriac
4 oz (100 g) onion
1 oz (25 g) butter
1¼ pt (750 ml) light stock
salt and pepper
3 tbs (45 ml) single cream
dash lemon juice
pinch dried dill

METHOD

Peel and slice the celeriac and onion. Melt the butter and sauté them gently for 1–2 minutes. Cover with damp greaseproof paper and a tight fitting lid. Cook gently for 10 minutes. Pour on stock and seasoning, bring to the boil and simmer for 30 minutes. Cool and blend before reheating. Away from the heat, stir in the cream, add a dash of lemon juice and dill. Season according to taste. After blending, the soup may be frozen. *Serves 3–4.*

Chip Buttie

RECIPE

2 thick slices of crusty white bread
½ oz (10 g) butter
freshly cooked chips
salt and pepper

METHOD

Spread both slices liberally with plenty of butter. Fill with sizzling hot, freshly fried chips, and season to taste. *Serves 1.*

TERRY WOGAN

EAT IMMEDIATELY!

33

VICTORIA WOOD

There is nothing like being able to unwind, after all that comedy, with a bit of 'serious stuff' on the radio!

Archers Soup

RECIPE

1 onion (chopped)
butter for frying
various vegetables (depending on taste)
vegetable stock cube

METHOD

Fry the onion in butter. Add any vegetables in the kitchen that aren't too revolting, chopped (and washed if you prefer). Chuck on some boiling water and a vegetable stock cube. Put the lid on. Listen to *The Archers*. Blend it a bit. Have it with toast.

Boozy Bolognese Sauce

RECIPE

2–3 tbs (30–45 ml) oil
1 onion (peeled and sliced)
1 red pepper (chopped)
4 oz (100 g) mushrooms (sliced)
8 oz (200 g) minced beef
salt and pepper
2 tbs (30 ml) tomato purée
¼ pt (125 ml) beef stock
3 tbs (45 ml) red wine

METHOD

Heat the oil and gently fry the onion, red pepper and mushrooms for 5 minutes or until soft. Add the minced beef and brown quickly, then lower the heat and add the seasoning, tomato purée, stock and wine. Bring to the boil, then lower the heat and simmer the sauce for 30 minutes.

Pour or spoon off any excess fat, then spoon the sauce over spaghetti or any other pasta, and serve. *Serves 4.*

ROBIN CASTLE (COXSWAIN)
SHEERNESS STATION,
ENGLAND
RNLB 'HELEN TURNBULL'
(Waveney class)

Curried Eggs

RECIPE

8 eggs (hard-boiled, halved)
2 large onions (peeled)
2 oz (50 g) butter
1 tbs (15 ml) each of flour, curry paste, tomato purée, chopped mango chutney
¾ pt (450 ml) chicken stock
1 tbs (15 ml) lemon juice
paprika
pinch of salt

METHOD

Arrange the hard-boiled eggs, cut side down, in a shallow dish. Slice the onion into rings and fry in butter until tender. Stir in the flour, curry paste, chutney, tomato purée, lemon juice and salt. Stir until smooth, then add the stock. Bring to the boil and simmer for 1 minute. Pour over the eggs and sprinkle with paprika. Cook at Gas Mark 4 or 350°F/180°C for 15 minutes. *Serves 4.*

Crispy Potato Skins

RECIPE

1½ lb (675 g) large potatoes (baked in the oven)
1 oz (25 g) butter
¼ pt (150 ml) soured cream (to serve)

METHOD

Remove the flesh from the potatoes, leaving a thin layer of skin, and reserve for another dish. Spread the potato skins with butter, put them on a baking sheet and cook in the oven for 20 minutes at Gas Mark 6 or 400°F/200°C, or under a high grill for 5–10 minutes, turning regularly, until they are crisp. Serve immediately with the soured cream.

"Make plenty, as these are always very popular. When cut into small pieces, they are excellent for a buffet."

CHRIS
BONINGTON

The Bonington Salad

RECIPE

*14 oz (400 g) can beans (eg red kidney, butter
beans, haricot, chick peas or flageolet)
1 lb (450 g) broccoli
1 small cauliflower (cut into florets)
4 oz (100 g) mushrooms (peeled and sliced)
½ bulb fennel (sliced)
2 carrots (peeled and finely chopped)
1 green pepper (de-seeded and sliced)
2 tomatoes (quartered)*

*1 oz (25 g) pumpkin seeds
1 tsp (5 ml) dried basil
1 tsp (5 ml) dried rosemary
olive oil
cider vinegar
black pepper
1 clove garlic (peeled and finely chopped –
optional)*

METHOD

Drain the beans, rinse, and put into a large salad bowl. Chop and
add raw vegetables and herbs. Mix in a dollop of olive oil and a dollop
of cider vinegar, some freshly ground black pepper to taste and I quite
like adding some chopped garlic, though this can be a little anti-social.
Finally, mix the whole lot up and have it with some wholemeal bread
and margarine or butter, and some really tasty cheese.

Butter Bean Casserole

RECIPE

8 oz (225 g) dried butter beans
20 shallots
2 oz (50 g) butter/margarine
1 tsp (5 ml) dried or chopped fresh savory
1 pt (600 ml) chicken stock
2–3 blades of mace
¼ pt (150 ml) plain yoghurt
freshly ground pepper
1 tbs (15 ml) chopped parsley

METHOD

Place the beans in a bowl, cover with boiling water and leave overnight. Blanch the shallots and take off the outer skin. Place the butter/margarine in a flameproof casserole and brown the shallots over a gentle heat. Add the beans, savory, mace and stock. Cook for $1\frac{1}{2}$–2 hours at Gas Mark 4 or 350°F/180°C, until the beans are tender and the stock is almost absorbed. Stir in the yoghurt and cook for a further 10 minutes. Sprinkle with chopped parsley and freshly ground pepper and serve. *Serves 4.*

SEBASTIAN COE

Seb likes to eat lots of pasta with a side salad; pasta for energy and salads for vitamin content. He also loves Italian food.

Tagliatelle alla Boscaiola

RECIPE

3 tbs (45 ml) olive oil
1 clove garlic (peeled and crushed)
14 oz (400 g) tin Italian plum tomatoes
salt and black pepper
1 tbs (15 ml) fresh basil or parsley (chopped)
8 oz (225 g) mushrooms (wiped and sliced)
1 lb (450 g) tagliatelle
2 oz (50 g) grated Parmesan cheese

METHOD

Heat 1 tbs (15 ml) oil in a saucepan, add the garlic and cook for a minute. Add the tomatoes and simmer for 5 minutes. Stir in the salt, pepper and basil or parsley.

Heat the remaining oil in a saucepan, add the mushrooms and cook gently for 3 minutes or until soft and beginning to colour.

Cook the tagliatelle in plenty of boiling salted water, according to packet instructions. Strain thoroughly, add the tomato sauce, stir, and turn into a heated serving dish. Spoon over the cooked mushrooms, sprinkle with cheese and serve immediately with a mixed green salad.

Serves 4.

Mushroom Roast

RECIPE

2 tbs (30 ml) oil
1 large onion (peeled and chopped)
½ red or green pepper (de-seeded and diced)
12 oz (350 g) flat mushrooms
4 oz (100 g) brown breadcrumbs
3 eggs, (beaten)
salt and pepper
8 oz (225 g) cheese (grated)
1 tbs (15 ml) parsley (chopped)

METHOD

Heat the oil in a frying pan, add the onion and cook for 5–6 minutes or until transparent. Add the diced pepper and continue cooking for 2 minutes, stirring occasionally. Add the mushrooms and cook for a further 2 minutes. Stir in the breadcrumbs, eggs, and salt and pepper. Spoon into an 8 in (20 cm) greased cake tin and sprinkle the grated cheese on top. Bake for 30–45 minutes at Gas Mark 7 or 425°F/220°C. Turn out of the tin and cut into wedges before serving, sprinkled with parsley. *Serves 4.*

SUE COOK

"I could happily live on a diet of big flat mushrooms, and since no-one in our family is a big meat-eater, this mushroom roast is quite a favourite. It is also a good vegetable dish to accompany meat or fish."

41

WENDY CRAIG

Potato Gratin

RECIPE

3 lb (1 kg 350 g) potatoes (peeled)
3 spring onions (sliced)
6 oz (175 g) Cheddar cheese (grated)
4 eggs (beaten)
1 clove garlic (peeled and crushed)
½ pt (300 ml) soured cream
salt and pepper

METHOD

Grate the potatoes into a colander and squeeze thoroughly with a paper towel to remove excess water. Mix with the spring onions, grated cheese, eggs, garlic and soured cream. Season to taste. Grease a shallow ovenproof baking dish and spoon in the mixture. Bake at Gas Mark 6 or 400°F/200°C for 40–45 minutes until crispy on top.
Serves 6–8.

Curry's Delight

RECIPE

2 tbs (30 ml) oil
2 cloves garlic (peeled and crushed)
1 small onion (peeled and sliced)
1 large carrot (sliced)
1 aubergine (trimmed and diced)
1 green pepper (de-seeded and sliced)
1 cauliflower (broken into florets)
1 tbs (15 ml) medium curry powder
½ pt (300 ml) vegetable stock

METHOD

Heat the oil in a large frying pan, add all the vegetables and cook for 5 minutes, stirring continuously. Stir in the curry powder, and cook for a further 2 minutes. Add the vegetable stock, bring to the boil, cover and simmer gently for approximately 20 minutes or until the vegetables are tender.

Serve with boiled brown rice. *Serves 4.*

MARK CURRY

A nice, simple-to-prepare dish from Mark – renowned for his lack of culinary expertise on *Blue Peter*!

A former single-handed sailor,
Clare is now a successful novelist.

Vegetable Lasagne

RECIPE

2 tbs (30 ml) oil
1 large onion (peeled and sliced)
8 oz (225 g) mushrooms (wiped and sliced)
1½ green peppers (de-seeded and chopped)
1 lb (450 g) aubergines (diced)
8 oz (225 g) courgettes (sliced – optional)
1 carrot (grated – optional)
14 oz (400 g) tin tomatoes
2 tbs (30 ml) tomato purée

½ pt (300 ml) vegetable stock
1 tsp (5 ml) dried mixed herbs, salt and pepper
14 oz (400 g) tin red kidney beans (drained)
½ pt (300 ml) béchamel sauce
2 oz (50 g) Cheddar or Mozarella cheese
(grated)
8 oz (225 g) pre-cooked lasagne
8 × 10 in (20 × 25 cm) lasagne dish or
roasting tin (greased)

METHOD

Heat the oil in a frying pan. Add the onion, mushrooms and peppers and cook gently for 5 minutes. Stir in the aubergine and courgettes and carrot, if using, and cook for a further 5 minutes. Add the tomatoes, tomato purée, vegetable stock and herbs. Stir and simmer, uncovered, for 8 minutes. Add the red kidney beans, salt and pepper.

Spoon a third of the vegetable sauce into the lasagne dish, then alternate with layers of lasagne, finishing with a layer of sauce. Top the dish with the béchamel sauce and sprinkle on the grated Cheddar of Mozarella cheese. Cook for 30–35 minutes at Gas Mark 6 or 400°F/200°C until the top is golden-brown and bubbling. Serves 4–6.

Glitter Fu-Yung

RECIPE

2 tbs (30 ml) oil
1 medium onion (peeled and chopped)
4 oz (100 g) mushrooms (wiped and sliced)
2 oz (50 g) peas
2 eggs (lightly beaten)
salt and freshly ground black pepper
pinch monosodium glutamate (optional)

METHOD

Heat the oil in a wok or deep frying pan. Add the onion and mushrooms and stir-fry for 3 minutes. Add the peas, then lower the heat and pour in the beaten eggs, salt, pepper and monosodium glutamate, if using. Scramble until the mixture is just set.
Pile onto a warmed plate and serve immediately. *Serves 1.*

GARY GLITTER

Gary likes this dish because it is quick and simple to prepare and, as it doesn't have any meat, it is suitable for vegetarians.

45

NERYS HUGHES

Leek Soufflé

RECIPE

4 leeks (white part only)
2 pt (1.2 l) water
large pinch salt
½ oz (10 g) butter
2 tbs (30 ml) dry breadcrumbs
2 tbs (30 ml) plain flour

12 fl oz (350 ml) milk
½ tsp (2.5 ml) each of salt, pepper and ground mace
3 egg yolks
3 egg whites

METHOD

Bring the water, salt and leeks to boil in a large pan, reduce the heat and cook for 12 minutes. Drain. Cool and slice thinly. Set the oven to Gas Mark 5 or 375°F/190°C. Grease a 2-pt (1.2 l) soufflé dish with half the butter and sprinkle the breadcrumbs on to the bottom and sides. Melt the remaining butter and stir in the flour to make a paste. Gradually add the milk, stirring constantly. Bring to the boil, beating till smooth. Remove from the heat, cool for 2 minutes, add the egg yolks and beat well. Season with salt, pepper and mace. Add the leeks and stir well until blended. Whisk the whites until stiff, then fold into the leek mixture. Gently pour into the prepared dish and bake for 20–25 minutes until puffy and brown. Serve at once. *Serves 4.*

Cheese Soufflé

RECIPE

1 oz (25 g) Parmesan cheese (grated)
1 ½ oz (30 g) butter
2 tbs (30 ml) plain flour
½ pt (300 ml) milk
4 egg yolks (beaten)

4 egg whites (beaten)
4 oz (100 g) Cheddar cheese (grated)
8 oz (225 g) frozen spinach (defrosted and chopped – optional)
salt, cayenne pepper, grated nutmeg

METHOD

Butter a 2 pt (1.2 l) soufflé dish and sprinkle Parmesan cheese inside. Melt the butter, stir in the flour and cook on a low heat for 1 minute. Add the milk and stir constantly. When the sauce has thickened, cook gently for a few minutes, then add the yolks, grated cheese and spinach, if using, and mix together. Season with salt, a pinch of cayenne and nutmeg. Remove from the heat and put into a large mixing bowl.

Mix a quarter of the egg whites into the mixture, then fold in the rest very quickly, taking care to keep the mixture fluffy. Transfer to the soufflé dish. Make a groove 1 in (2.5 cm) from the edge of the mixture with your thumb and cook for 35–40 minutes (depending on texture preferred) at Gas Mark 6 or 400°F/200°C until the top is golden brown. Do not open the door while cooking!

NIGEL LAWSON

VIRGINIA McKENNA

"When I lived in the Sudan, aubergines were very much part of the staple diet, starting with aubergine jam for breakfast and finishing with aubergine stew at night. This dish is one of my favourite ways of eating them and is delicious served with steamed courgettes, broccoli and tomato sauce."

Vegetable Moussaka

RECIPE

1 pt (600 ml) water
4 tbs (60 ml) olive oil
2 oz (50 g) green or brown lentils
1 onion (peeled and chopped)
1 clove garlic (crushed)
4 oz (100 g) mushrooms (chopped)
3 tbs (45 ml) tomato purée
2 tsp (10 ml) dried oregano

1 tsp (5 ml) freshly grated nutmeg
salt and freshly ground black pepper
12 oz (350 g) aubergines (washed and sliced)
2 tomatoes (washed and thickly sliced)
2 potatoes (scrubbed, boiled and sliced)
½ pt (300 ml) white sauce
3 oz (75 g) grated Cheddar cheese

METHOD

Wash the lentils, bring to the boil in the water then cover and simmer for 40–45 minutes. Drain and reserve the liquid. Heat 2 tbs (30 ml) oil and fry the onion and garlic gently so they remain translucent. Add the mushrooms and lentils and cook for a few minutes, mixing well. Remove vegetables to a bowl and mix in a little lentil liquid, tomato purée and the oregano. Season with nutmeg, salt and pepper. Add the remaining oil to the pan and fry the aubergine slices until soft, turning constantly. Put the slices on a piece of kitchen paper to drain and let them cool. Grease a 3 pt (1·75 l) ovenproof dish. Put in a layer of lentil and mushroom mixture, then aubergines, then potato and tomato slices. Pour on the white sauce and sprinkle with the cheese. Bake at Gas Mark 4 or 350°F/180°C for 40 minutes until the cheese is golden brown and bubbling. Serves 4.

Buckwheat Burgers

RECIPE

1 large onion (peeled and chopped)
1 tbs (15 ml) sesame oil
4 oz (100 g) buckwheat
12 fl oz (350 ml) water
1 tsp (5 ml) light tahini
3 tsp (15 ml) vinegar (preferably *umeboshi)

6 tbs (90 ml) parsley (chopped)
6 oz (175 g) whole wheat breadcrumbs
sesame oil for frying

* umeboshi is a Japanese pickled plum

METHOD

Sauté the onion in oil for 3 minutes. Add the buckwheat and sauté for 5 to 10 minutes, or until golden brown. Add the water, bring to boil and simmer gently for 20 minutes. Turn off the heat and let stand, covered, for 10 minutes. Mix tahini and vinegar, pour into the buckwheat, add the parsley and stir well. Cover and let cool. The mixture should be soft and sticky. Wet your hands and shape the mixture into 4 to 6 croquettes and roll these in breadcrumbs.

Heat a little sesame oil in a frying pan and gently sauté the burgers on both sides until brown. Serve with parsley sauce and watercress and orange salad.

KEITH MICHELL

You can buy some of these ingredients at any good Health Food store and for further recipes, Keith Michell has written a book called *Practically Macrobiotic* published by Thorsons Publishing Group, price £8.99.

DESMOND
MORRIS

"We discovered this recipe when we were living in Malta. Our local cook made the following dish from artichokes, which we grew in our garden. It is full of the sunshine found in the Mediterranean – piquant and delicious."

Stuffed Artichokes,
Maltese Fashion

RECIPE

4 globe artichokes
4 anchovy fillets (cut into small pieces)
1 clove garlic (finely chopped)
1 tbs (15 ml) each of chopped chives and chopped parsley
4 olives (chopped into small pieces)
4 oz (100 g) breadcrumbs
salt and pepper
6 tbs (90 ml) olive oil
2 tbs (30 ml) vinegar

METHOD

Soak the artichokes in salted water for 30 minutes, drain and beat each one, face down, on a work surface, so the leaves open a little. Prepare the filling by mixing together the anchovies, garlic, chives, parsley, olives, breadcrumbs, salt and pepper. Moisten the mixture with half the olive oil. Fill the artichokes with the mixture between the leaves. Place them, packed together, in a saucepan. Pour the remaining oil and vinegar over each artichoke, add a little water to the pan, cover closely and simmer gently for 2 hours or more until the leaves come off easily when pulled. Serve with crusty bread.

Shipboard Eggs

RECIPE

1 lb (450 g) tomatoes (skinned and chopped)
1 large onion (chopped)
6 tbs (90 ml) oil
½ tsp (2·5 ml) dried basil
1 tsp (5 ml) tomato purée

6 eggs (separated)
3 oz (75 g) Parmesan cheese (freshly grated)
3 tbs (45 ml) plain flour
salt and freshly-milled black pepper

METHOD

Heat 2 tbs (30 ml) oil in a medium-sized saucepan, then add the chopped onion and cook over a medium heat for 5 minutes or so until soft but not brown. Add the chopped tomatoes and the basil, cover the pan and cook over a fairly low heat for 30 minutes. Stir in the tomato purée and season with salt and freshly-milled pepper. Keep the sauce warm.

In the frying pan, heat a further 2 tbs (30 ml) of oil. Place the egg whites in a mixing bowl and whisk until stiff but not dry. Then combine the Parmesan cheese and the flour together with a little season-ing, and fold this into the egg whites.

Pre-heat the grill. Drop tablespoons of the batter mixture into the hot oil in the frying pan, to get 6 fritters in all. When golden brown on the underside, flip them over to cook on the other side. Arrange the fritters on a warmed serving dish, spoon a little tomato sauce over each one, make a slight indentation in the sauce with the spoon, then slip an egg yolk on top of each fritter.

Grill briefly to set the egg yolk and serve immediately accompanied by some crusty bread. *Serves 3.*

DELIA SMITH

"I'm no sailor, but having seen a few ships' galleys, I can see why they call for such ingenuity. They are usually so small that only the barest essentials can be stored. So it probably won't surprise you to learn that this recipe was the invention of a long-distance sailor."

MARGARET THATCHER

Margaret Thatcher

Courgettes Maison

RECIPE

4 courgettes
2 oz (50 g) butter
1 shallot (peeled and finely chopped)
2 tbs (30 ml) plain flour
¼ pt (150 ml) milk
4 tomatoes (peeled and chopped)
2 oz (50 g) cheese (grated)
4 oz (100 g) prawns (peeled)
salt and pepper

METHOD

Blanch the courgettes whole until tender. Melt the butter in a saucepan, add the shallot and cook for 5 minutes until soft. Stir in the flour, then gradually add the milk. Bring to the boil and simmer for 2 minutes. Scald and skin the tomatoes, quarter and remove seeds. Cut the courgettes in half. Scoop out the flesh and mix into the sauce with the chopped tomatoes, 1 oz (25 g) of the cheese, prawns, salt and pepper. Replace the mixture in the courgette skins, sprinkle with grated cheese and brown under a moderate grill. *Serves 4.*

Crunchy Salad

RECIPE

½ iceberg lettuce
½ cucumber
4 tomatoes
2 sticks celery (wiped)
2 apples (cored)
1 green pepper
1 red pepper
4 oz (100 g) beansprouts
2 oz (50 g) mixed nuts (chopped)
2 oz (50 g) raisins
4 oz (100 g) Cambozola cheese

METHOD

Slice the lettuce, cucumber, tomatoes, celery and apples and place in a large salad bowl. De-seed and slice the peppers and add with the beansprouts, nuts and raisins. Mix well. Cut the cheese into cubes and scatter over the top of the salad. Serve with wholemeal bread.
Serves 4.

SUSANNAH YORK

There is plenty of scope with this recipe for adding different vegetables or any other flavourings you may like the taste of. Susannah's favourite pasta for this dish is green tagliatelle.

My Pasta (Pasta Casa Nostra)

RECIPE

2 lbs (30 ml) olive oil
2 or 3 cloves garlic (peeled and crushed)
1 onion (peeled and chopped)
1 lb (450 g) tomatoes (peeled and chopped), or 14 oz (400 g) tin tomatoes
1 green pepper (de-seeded and chopped)
2 tbs (30 ml) tomato purée
2 bay leaves
1 tbs (15 ml) fresh chopped or 1 tsp (5 ml)

dried oregano, black olives (stoned)
salt and freshly ground pepper
½ red pepper (de-seeded and chopped – optional)
8 oz (225 g) button mushrooms (wiped and sliced – optional)
4 fl oz (100 ml) red or white wine (optional)
1 lb (450 g) fresh pasta
2 oz (50 g) Cheddar or Parmesan cheese

METHOD

Heat one tsp (5 ml) olive oil in a large saucepan. Add the garlic and onion and cook gently until soft. Add the tomatoes, green pepper, tomato purée, bay leaves, oregano, black olives, salt and pepper, red pepper, mushrooms and wine, if liked. Simmer, uncovered, for 10 minutes. Remove bay leaves. Cook the pasta in boiling salted water, to which the remaining oil has been added, for 3–5 minutes or until just cooked, *al dente*. Drain thoroughly and serve with the vegetable sauce, sprinkled with plenty of freshly grated cheese. *Serves 5–6.*

Steak Diane

RECIPE

4 pieces fillet steak
1 oz (25 g) butter
2 tbs (30 ml) oil
2 tbs (30 ml) Worcestershire sauce
1 tbs (15 ml) lemon juice
1 tbs (15 ml) grated onion
2 tbs (30 ml) chopped parsley

METHOD

Fry the steaks in the butter and oil for 1 to 2 minutes each side.
Remove them from the pan and keep warm. Add the Worcestershire
sauce and lemon juice to the juices in the pan. Stir well and warm
through. Add the onion and parsley and cook gently for 1 minute.
Spoon the sauce over the steak and serve. *Serves 4.*

DESMOND ROGERS
(CHIEF HELMSMAN)
PORTAFERRY STATION,
NORTHERN IRELAND
RNLB 'BLUE PETER – V'
(Atlantic 21 class)

JEFFREY ARCHER

"I like fish when it's done properly. This is an excellent meal, but don't eat too much – it can be fattening."

Creamed Seafood Bake

RECIPE

2 tbs (30 ml) oil
8 oz (225 g) long grain brown rice
1 pt (600 ml) boiling water
½ onion (finely chopped)
3 oz (75 g) raisins
1½ lb (675 g) mixed seafood (prawns, halibut, scallops, etc)
4 oz (100 g) mushrooms (sliced)
4 oz (100 g) butter

2 tsp (10 ml) fresh root ginger (grated)
2 tsp (10 ml) hot curry powder
3 fl oz (75 ml) dry sherry
1 oz (25 g) plain flour
½ tsp (2.5 ml) mustard powder
½ pt (300 ml) single cream
4 oz (100 g) Cheddar cheese (grated)
pinch of cayenne pepper
salt and black pepper

METHOD

Heat oil in frying pan. Add the rice and onions and cook for 5 minutes. Add raisins and water, bring to the boil, cover and simmer for 40 minutes until tender. Meanwhile, melt 2 oz (50 g) of the butter, fry the mushrooms for 2 to 3 minutes, remove from pan, then add another 1 oz (25 g) of butter to the pan and add seafood and sherry. Cook for 5 minutes then remove and add to mushrooms. Reserve pan juices.

Add remaining butter to the pan. Stir in flour, ginger, curry powder and mustard powder. Add the pan juices, cream, salt and pepper, stir and cook until thickened. Pour over fish and mushrooms. Arrange the rice in a baking dish. Spoon the fish mixture over, sprinkle with cheese and cayenne pepper and bake at Gas Mark 6 or 400°F/200°C for 30 minutes. *Serves 4–6.*

Gratin of Crab with a Curry Sabayon

SARAH BRIGHTMAN

RECIPE

4 × 1½ lb (675 g) crabs (cooked and dressed)
2 tsp (10 ml) oil
1 shallot (peeled and chopped)
1 tbs (15 ml) medium curry powder
3 egg yolks

4 fl oz (100 ml) whipping or double cream
salt and freshly ground black pepper
dash lemon juice
8 oz (225 g) beansprouts

METHOD

Remove the meat from the shells. Lightly flake the white meat and reserve.

Heat the oil in a saucepan, add the shallot and cook for 3 minutes or until soft. Stir in the curry powder and cook for a further minute. Place in a food processor with the brown crab meat and purée until smooth. Press the mixture through a fine sieve.

Whisk the egg yolks in a bowl over a pan of very hot water until the yolks are thick and light. Fold into the puréed brown crab meat. Whip the cream until soft peaks form. Fold into the mixture. Taste and add salt, pepper and lemon juice to taste.

Blanch the beansprouts for 1 minute in boiling water, then rinse under cold running water. Mix with the white crab-meat and spoon into the shells. Pour the curry sauce over.

Bake at Gas Mark 4 or 350°F/180°C for 15 minutes. Serve immediately. *Serves 4.*

Frank's Knuckle-Duster

RECIPE

1 oz (25 g) butter or margarine
1 medium onion (finely chopped)
1 lb (450 g) minced beef
2 oz (50 g) fresh breadcrumbs
4 tbs (60 ml) HP sauce
1 egg (beaten)
salt and pepper

METHOD

Grease and line a 1 lb (450 g) loaf tin. Melt the butter in a frying pan, add the onion and cook until softened. Turn into a large bowl. Add the remaining ingredients and stir until evenly mixed. Spoon the mixture into the loaf tin, level the surface and cover tightly with foil. Stand the loaf tin in a roasting tin and pour in water to a depth of 1 in (2·5 cm). Bake in the oven at Gas Mark 4 or 350°F/180°C for $1\frac{1}{2}$ hours. Turn out and serve. Can be eaten hot or cold. *Serves 4.*

Family Turkey Pie

RECIPE

12 oz (350 g) rough puff or shortcrust pastry
2 oz (50 g) streaky bacon
1 medium onion (chopped)
1 oz (25 g) margarine
1 oz (25 g) plain flour
¼ pt (150 ml) turkey stock or chicken stock

¼ pt (150 ml) milk
8 oz (225 g) cooked turkey (chopped)
1 tbs (15 ml) lemon juice
pinch nutmeg
salt and pepper
beaten egg to glaze

METHOD

De-rind the bacon and fry the rinds to extract fat. Remove the rinds from the pan, add the bacon, cut into small pieces and chopped onion. Fry until lightly browned. Keep hot. Melt the margarine in a pan, and stir in the flour. Gradually add the stock and milk and bring to the boil – stirring all the time. Add the turkey, bacon, onion, lemon juice, nutmeg, salt and pepper and stir well. Allow to cool. Roll out a little more than half the pastry and line an 8 in (20 cm) pie dish. Spoon in the filling, then roll out the remaining pastry to form a lid. Dampen the edge of the bottom layer of pastry, then top with the lid. Brush top with beaten egg. Bake at Gas Mark 6 or 400°F/200°C for about 30 minutes, just above the centre of the oven. *Serves 4–6.*

BRIAN CLOUGH

"I personally enjoy cooking very much, and this is a recipe which I both enjoy making and eating. A good, filling pie, and one which I find very useful after Christmas!"

JACKIE
COLLINS

"Living in Hollywood, I find that
everyone loves Shepherd's Pie –
it reminds them of home!"

Shepherd's Pie

RECIPE

2 lb (900 g) lean ground beef
2 medium onions (peeled and chopped)
2 large carrots (peeled and chopped)
1 beef stock cube
10 oz (275 g) can condensed tomato soup
10 fl oz (300 ml) water
salt, pepper and mixed herbs
6 large potatoes
1 oz (25 g) butter

METHOD

Fry beef without extra fat. Remove from pan with slotted spoon
and set aside. Add onions and cook for 3 minutes. Add carrots, soup,
water and beef cube to mixture. Simmer for 5 minutes. Add a smattering
of salt, black pepper and mixed herbs, then stir in cooked meat and
transfer to a deep oven dish.

Boil and mash potatoes until creamy. Place on top of meat mixture
and dot with butter. Cook at Gas Mark 5 or 375°F/190°C for 1 hour.
Serves 4–6.

Ragù Bolognese

RECIPE

2 oz (50 g) butter
4 oz (100 g) smoked ham (finely chopped)
1 medium onion and 2 carrots (peeled and finely chopped)
2 sticks celery (wiped and finely chopped)
2 tbs (30 ml) olive oil
12 oz (350 g) minced beef
12 oz (350 g) lean minced pork

4 fl oz (100 ml) dry white wine
15 fl oz (450 ml) beef stock
2 tbs (30 ml) tomato purée
8 oz (225 g) chicken livers
4 fl oz (100 ml) double cream
pinch ground nutmeg
salt and freshly ground black pepper
cooked pasta of choice

METHOD

Heat half the butter in a frying pan. Add the ham, onion, carrots and celery, and cook, stirring frequently until lightly browned. Transfer to a large heavy saucepan. Heat the oil in the frying pan, add the minced beef and pork and cook over a moderate heat until the meat is brown. Add the wine, increase the heat and boil briskly until the liquid has almost evaporated. Add to the saucepan with the stock and tomato purée. Bring to the boil and simmer, uncovered, for 40 minutes, stirring occasionally.

Meanwhile, heat the remaining butter in the frying pan, add the chicken livers and cook for 2–3 minutes or until brown and firm. Chop and add to the sauce 5 minutes before the end of cooking. Stir in the cream, nutmeg, salt and pepper. Serve with pasta.

TOM CONTI

"There is no tidy way to eat spaghetti. You must forget that you are British. Wind some on to the fork and put it in your mouth. Bite off the hanging bits and let them fall back on to the plate, you'll get them next time. Don't let silly things like 'table manners' spoil your enjoyment of one of the world's truly great dishes. Drink red wine with this – unless you're driving. Soda with a dash of lime cordial seems to go very well."

Pasta alla Amatriciana

RECIPE

2 tbs (30 ml) olive oil
12 rashers unsmoked bacon (chopped)
1 clove garlic
2 medium sized onions (finely chopped)
thyme

2 14-oz (400 g) tins tomatoes
¼ pt (150 ml) chicken stock
black pepper
Parmigiano (Parmesan) cheese for grating
1 ¼ lb (550 g) dried pasta

METHOD

Fry the bacon in oil then remove and keep warm. Peel the garlic, lay the flat of a knife blade on top and give it a thump with your fist. After you've bandaged your hand, add the split clove to the oil and sauté. After a few moments *discard* it. Garlic is a natural flavour enhancer; neither the dish nor you should reek of it! Now add the onions to the oil and sprinkle with a pinch of thyme and sauté. Before the onions burn, add the tomatoes. Do not pour them straight from the tin but first crush them. Add chicken stock to the pan and season with black pepper – but no salt, the stock cube supplies that. Simmer gently without a lid for 10–15 minutes until fairly thick, stirring occasionally. Stir in the bacon. Grate in some cheese and stir. Cook the pasta of your choice *al dente* (slightly firm at the centre) in 8–12 pts (3–7 l) salted water. Spoon the sauce over the pasta and serve with extra grated Parmesan and black pepper.

Beefsteak & Kidney Pie

RECIPE

1½ lb (675 g) chuck steak (cubed)
6 oz (175 g) ox kidney (chopped)
½ lb (225 g) dark-gilled mushrooms (sliced)
2 medium onions (peeled and chopped)
1 tbs (15 ml) flour
1 tbs (15 ml) beef dripping

¾ pt (450 ml) beef stock
½ tsp (2·5 ml) Worcestershire sauce
2 tsp (10 ml) mushroom ketchup
½ tsp (2·5 ml) dried mixed herbs
salt and freshly-milled black pepper
6 oz (175 g) shortcrust pastry

METHOD

Fry the chopped onion in the dripping in a large saucepan for a few minutes, then add the cubes of steak and kidney. Continue to cook (stirring occasionally) until the meat is nicely browned, then add the flour and stir it in well. Add the herbs, Worcestershire sauce and ketchup. Season with salt and pepper and gradually stir in the stock. Finally, add the mushrooms, cover and simmer gently for about 2 hours, or until the meat is tender. When cooked, check the seasoning and pour everything into an oval pie-dish.

Roll out the pastry on a lightly-floured surface to make a lid and a 1 in (2·5 cm) strip to line the inside edge of the pie-dish. Press this pastry strip on, dampen it and lay the pastry lid on top, pressing it down and sealing it around the edge. Flute the edge, make a small steam-hole in the centre, and bake at Gas Mark 7 or 425°F/220°C for 25–30 minutes, until the pastry is golden brown. *Serves 4–6.*

HENRY COOPER

"Although I eat out quite a lot, I prefer homemade food because it's wholesome and good."

ANDY
CRANE

"I like lasagne because it is tasty, quick to cook and always fills me up; especially when served with a salad and chips!"

Lasagne

RECIPE

8 oz (225 g) lasagne verde
1 tbs (15 ml) oil
15 oz (425 g) tin minced beef
1 tbs (15 ml) tomato purée
¼ tsp (1 ml) garlic salt
pinch black pepper
¼ pt (150 ml) single cream
2 oz (50 g) grated cheese

METHOD

Cook the lasagne in a large pan of boiling salted water to which the oil has been added. Allow 3 minutes for fresh, 8 minutes for dried pasta. Drain and keep hot. Empty the meat into a saucepan with the tomato purée, garlic salt and black pepper to taste. Cook for 5 minutes, stirring occasionally. Arrange the lasagne and meat in layers in a lightly-greased ovenproof dish, finishing with a layer of meat. Cover the dish and cook at Gas Mark 6 or 400°F/200°C for 15 minutes.

Remove the cover and pour cream over top. Sprinkle with cheese and return to the oven for a further 10 minutes, or brown under a hot grill for 3–4 minutes. Serve immediately. *Serves 4.*

Cardamom Fish Curry

RECIPE

1 ½ lb (625 g) white fish
1 green chilli
2 cloves garlic
1 in (2·5 cm) piece fresh ginger
2 tbs (30 ml) sunflower oil
1 medium red pepper (thinly sliced)

3 oz (75 g) creamed coconut
2 tsp (10 ml) salt
½ pt (300 ml) boiling water
juice 1 lemon
6 cardamom pods
1 tbs (15 ml) freshly chopped parsley

METHOD

Cut the fish into large chunks. Cut the chilli open and de-seed. Peel the garlic and ginger, and chop them together finely.

Heat the oil in a large casserole. Stir in the chilli, garlic and ginger, plus the cardamom pods. Add the fish and cook for a few minutes on each side to seal. Add the red pepper and remove from the heat.

Put the coconut and salt into a measuring jug, add the boiling water and stir. Pour over the fish. Add the lemon juice. Bring to a gentle boil, cover and cook at Gas Mark 3 or 325°F/170°C for 30–40 minutes. Sprinkle the parsley over before serving. *Serves 4–5.*

SIR COLIN DAVIS

"This must be served with basmati rice, very carefully prepared to enjoy it at its best."

SIR ROBIN DAY

A typical dish from the Victorian era when breakfast was an elaborate affair. Of Indian origin, 'Khichari' consisted of rice with fish, lentils, onion, fresh limes and spices.

Kedgeree

RECIPE

1½ lb (675 g) thick smoked haddock fillets
3 oz (75 g) butter
1 onion chopped
½ in (1·2 cm) piece fresh root ginger (peeled and grated)

½ red pepper (de-seeded and chopped)
½ green pepper (de-seeded and chopped)
6 oz (175 g) long-grain rice
2 hard-boiled eggs
salt and freshly ground black pepper

METHOD

Place the haddock fillets in a saucepan and cover with 1 pt (600 ml) cold water. Bring to the boil, cover and simmer for 8 minutes. Drain off the liquid and reserve. Remove the haddock fillets and reserve.

Melt 2 oz (50 g) of the butter in the same saucepan, add the onion and cook for 5 minutes. Add the ginger, peppers and rice, then pour over 15 fl oz (450 ml) of the reserved fish liquor. Stir once, bring to the boil, cover and simmer gently for 15 minutes or until the rice is tender and the liquid absorbed.

Meanwhile, remove the skin and bones from the fish and flake. Peel and chop the hard-boiled eggs. When the rice is cooked, stir in the fish, eggs, seasoning and remaining butter. Heat through for 2 minutes, then transfer to a hot serving dish. *Serves 4.*

Poached Salmon

RECIPE

1 whole salmon
1 fresh lemon
freshly ground black pepper

METHOD

Clean the fish, then squeeze fresh lemon juice over it and a good quantity of freshly ground black pepper. Wrap in foil.

Bring a fish kettle of water to the boil, add the fish, and continue simmering very gently for 2 minutes only. Remove the pan from the heat and leave in a cool place. The salmon continues to cook in the hot water and this keeps it moist. When the water is hand-hot, the fish will be cooked. If serving the salmon cold, remove it and leave wrapped in foil to keep moist. Store in the refrigerator. Serve with a sauce of your choice.

This method works well for any size fish, so long as the fish kettle is roughly the right size. (A small fish in a large kettle would be overcooked by the time it came to the boil.)

ANNE DIAMOND

Pork & Parsnips

RECIPE

1½ lb (675 g) lean pork (cubed)
2 tsp (10 ml) coarsely crushed coriander seeds
2 tbs (30 ml) oil
1 large onion (peeled and chopped)
2 tbs (30 ml) plain flour
2 tsp (10 ml) Dijon mustard
¾ pt (450 ml) chicken stock
1 bay leaf
1 lb (450 g) parsnips (peeled and cut into chunks)
2 tbs (30 ml) chopped parsley
salt and pepper

METHOD

Heat the oil and brown the pork with the coriander seeds. Add the onion and cook gently for 3 to 4 minutes. Stir in the flour, mustard and stock with the bay leaf. Bring to the boil and allow to simmer for 15 minutes.

Add the parsnips and continue to simmer gently for 30 minutes or until tender. Remove the bay leaf. Stir in the chopped parsley, salt and pepper before serving. *Serves 4.*

Traditional Lancashire Hot Pot

RECIPE

4 mutton chops (trimmed)
3 lamb's kidneys (skinned, cored and sliced)
1 lb (450 g) onions (sliced) or small pickling onions
2 lb (900 g) potatoes (peeled and sliced)
¾ pt (450 ml) home-made rich beef stock
2 oz (50 g) dripping or butter
salt and pepper

METHOD

Place chops in a deep earthenware casserole, and add alternate layers of kidney, onions and potatoes, ending with a layer of potatoes. Season the stock to taste and pour over. Dot the top with dripping. Cover and cook at Gas Mark 3 or 325°F/160°C, for about 2½–3 hours or until the meat is tender. Remove the lid for the last 30 minutes to brown the topping. Serve with red cabbage. *Serves 4.*

BETTY DRIVER

Betty Turpin from *Coronation Street* Lunchtime regulars at *Coronation Street*'s Rovers Return just can't get enough of Betty Turpin's Traditional Hot Pot. However, if you want to be posh, like the Bolton folk, you can add some oysters and mushrooms and call it Bolton Hot Pot.

MICHAEL FISH

Lo Manazatti

RECIPE

1 oz (25 g) margarine
2 lb (900 g) lean pork fillet (cubed)
8 onions (peeled and sliced)
4 oz (100 g) tomato purée
¾ lb (350 g) mushrooms (sliced)
15 oz (425 g) tin condensed mushroom soup
2 green peppers (de-seeded and sliced)
6 oz (175 g) mature Cheddar cheese
salt and cayenne pepper
2 lb (900 g) packet pasta shells

METHOD

Melt half the margarine, add the onions and cook for 5 minutes or until soft. Spoon into a large casserole. Heat the remaining margarine and fry the pork until well-browned. Remove from the pan and put with the onions.

Stir in all the other ingredients, except the pasta and cheese. Cook the pasta in boiling, salted water for 8 minutes. Drain well and add to the mixture and stir to combine all ingredients. Grate cheese over the top. Cover and cook at Gas Mark 4 or 350°F/180°C for 1 hour, or until the meat is tender.

Whole Fish on the Spit

RECIPE

3 lb (1·4 kg) fish (cod, saithe or bream),
cleaned with head and tail removed
½ tsp (2·5 ml) paprika
4 tbs (60 ml) coriander
6 cardamom pods
1 tbs (15 ml) aniseed or dill
2 onions (chopped)
2 cloves garlic (crushed)

2 tbs (30 ml) mint (chopped)
4 tbs (60 ml) parsley (chopped)
1 green pepper (sliced)
5 fl oz (150 ml) yoghurt
juice of 1 lemon or lime
salt and pepper
2 oz (50 g) ghee (clarified butter)

METHOD

Roast the paprika and coriander in a frying pan, then place in a food processor together with the other spices, onions, garlic, herbs, green pepper, yoghurt and lemon juice, and blend to a smooth paste.

Prick the fish all over and rub the mixture all over it. Season with salt and pepper, cover and leave to marinate for 1 hour.

Put the fish on a spit or under the grill with a drip tray to catch the juices. Cook for about 15 minutes until the paste is dry. Baste with the juices from the pan and cook for a further 25 minutes over a gentle heat. Turn once during cooking. When the flesh flakes easily, it is cooked. Raise the heat, baste the fish with the ghee and cook until the skin is crisp. Serve at once. *Serves 2–3.*

TERESA GORMAN

Hawaiian Chicken

RECIPE

4 chicken joints (skinned)
1 tbs (15 ml) cornflour
2 tbs (30 ml) light brown sugar
2 tbs (30 ml) white wine vinegar
2 tbs (30 ml) light soy sauce
salt and pepper
8 oz (225 g) tin pineapple pieces in syrup
8 maraschino cherries (stoned)

METHOD

Arrange the chicken pieces in a casserole dish. In a small saucepan mix the cornflour, sugar, vinegar, soy sauce, salt and pepper to a smooth paste. Stir in the juice from the tin of pineapples. Cook the mixture until thickened, stirring all the time. Pour over the chicken and cook at Gas Mark 4, or 350°F/180°C for $1\frac{1}{4}$–$1\frac{1}{2}$ hours, or until the chicken is tender – the flavour will penetrate the chicken.

Stir in the pineapple pieces and cherries just before serving. Can be served hot or cold. *Serves 4.*

Steak and Kidney Pud

RECIPE

For the pastry
8 oz (225 g) plain flour
4 oz (100 g) shredded suet
½ tsp (2.4 ml) salt
cold water
For the filling
1 lb (450 g) chuck steak (cubed)
4 oz (100 g) ox kidney (cut up)

seasoned flour
beef dripping for frying
2 onions (peeled and chopped)
For the gravy
2 beef stock cubes
1 tsp (5 ml) each of Worcestershire sauce and
Marmite
1 pt (600 ml) hot water

METHOD

Mix flour, suet and salt and add enough cold water to make a dough. Allow to rest before rolling out.

Roll the steak and kidney in seasoned flour and gently fry in beef dripping to seal in flavour. Fry the onions for about a minute.

Roll out pastry and line a 2 pt (1 l) basin, leaving enough pastry to make a lid. Put in the steak, kidney and onions and pour in gravy, but not enough to fill the basin. Put on the pastry lid and seal the edges well. Cover with greaseproof paper and kitchen foil and steam for 4 to 5 hours.

Serve with mashed spuds and cabbage. *Serves 4.*

RUSSELL GRANT

Astrologer Russell Grant predicts that this dish will go down great with your guests. It is one of his favourite dishes and is good old English fare. However, you mustn't be in a hurry to eat: it takes some hours to cook to perfection.

73

JIMMY GREAVES

Beef Goulash

RECIPE

1 lb (450 g) stewing beef
2 tbs (30 ml) oil
2 onions (peeled and sliced)
1 tbs (15 ml) paprika
¼ pt (150 ml) beef stock
salt and pepper
2 tbs (30 ml) tomato purée
2 lb (900 g) potatoes
¼ pt (150 ml) soured cream

METHOD

Cut the meat into cubes and fry in the oil until brown. Add the sliced onion and cook until brown. Stir in the paprika, then add the stock, salt, pepper and tomato purée. Bring to the boil, reduce the heat, cover and simmer for 2 hours. Add the potatoes cut in quarters and simmer for 20 minutes. Stir in the cream just before serving. Serve hot with rice. *Serves 4.*

Chicken Stuffed With Asparagus

& Lime Mousse With Cream Lemon Sauce

RECIPE

4 boneless chicken supremes (skinned)
4 fresh asparagus spears
1 egg
¼ pt (150 ml) double cream
salt and freshly ground pepper
finely grated rind of 1 lime

For the sauce
½ pt (300 ml) double cream
2 tbs (30 ml) white wine
juice 1 lemon
finely grated rind ½ lemon
1 tbs (15 ml) chopped parsley

METHOD

Trim the tips from the asparagus and reserve. Place the remainder in a food processor, with the egg, double cream, seasoning and lime rind and purée until smooth. Spoon the purée into the supreme cavities and loosely wrap each in greased foil. Place on a baking tray and bake at Gas Mark 4 or 350°F/180°C for 20–25 minutes, or until chicken is cooked. Place the wine and lemon juice in a small pan, bring to the boil and simmer until reduced by one third. Gradually stir in the cream. Taste and adjust seasoning if necessary. Add the asparagus tips and heat in the sauce until tender. Serve the chicken coated with sauce and garnished with the asparagus tips from the sauce, a sprinkling of lemon rind and chopped parsley. *Serves 4.*

SIR RALPH HALPERN

75

JEREMY HANLEY

"Here is one of my normally over-indulgent recipes, and since I love cooking I can assure you that it works. Mind, it took two or three attempts, but now it is perfect every time."

Yorkshire Surprise

RECIPE

3 oz (75 g) plain flour
1 egg
5 fl oz (125 ml) milk
salt and pepper
2 tbs (30 ml) cold water
1 oz (25 g) butter
1 clove garlic (peeled and crushed – optional)
3 tbs (45 ml) brandy
3 6–8 oz (175–225 g) fillet steaks

METHOD

To make the batter, sift the flour into a mixing bowl, make a well in the centre, break the egg in and gradually mix in the milk, water and seasoning. Leave to stand for a few minutes. Melt the butter and seal the steaks in a hot frying pan, adding garlic, if using, and the brandy. When the steaks are browned all over, put them into metal steak and kidney pudding bowls. Thicker, narrower steaks are preferable to thinner, flatter ones. Pour the batter around the steaks and put the bowls into the oven for about 25 minutes at Gas Mark 7 or 425°F/220°C. Do not open the oven until at least 20 minutes have passed. *Serves 3.*

Chicken Woodcote

RECIPE

8 chicken thighs
3 tbs (45 ml) olive oil
8 oz (225 g) button mushrooms
1 glass white wine
7 oz (200 g) tin tomatoes (chopped)
1 clove garlic (crushed)
¼ pt (150 ml) chicken stock
salt and pepper
1 tbs (15 ml) chopped parsley

METHOD

Sauté the chicken in the olive oil. Add the mushrooms and cook slowly together for 20–25 minutes with the lid on, turning occasionally. When cooked, remove the chicken and mushrooms to a fireproof dish to keep warm. Add the wine, tomatoes, garlic, stock, salt and pepper to the pan and cook over a high heat for 8–10 minutes to reduce the sauce. Stir occasionally to prevent sticking. Strain the sauce over the chicken and sprinkle with chopped parsley. *Serves 4.*

EDWARD HEATH

LENNY HENRY

Paprika Chicken

RECIPE

4 chicken joints
2 tbs (30 ml) vegetable oil
1 oz (25 g) butter
1 onion (peeled and chopped)
2 tbs (30 ml) paprika
1 oz (25 g) flour
¼ pt (150 ml) dry cider

¼ pt (150 ml) stock
5 tbs (75 ml) sherry
1 tsp (5 ml) tomato purée
6 oz (175 g) mushrooms
¼ pt (150 ml) cream
salt and pepper

METHOD

Remove the skin from chicken. Heat the oil in pan, add the butter and fry the chicken till light brown. Remove from the pan, add the onion and paprika and fry for 2 minutes. Stir in the flour and cook for a further minute. Remove from the heat and stir in the stock, cider and sherry, then return to the heat and simmer until thick. Add the tomato purée and seasoning to the sauce. Stir well, return the chicken to the sauce, cover and cook until the chicken is tender, turning once. Add the mushrooms and cook for a further 5 minutes. When ready to serve, lift the chicken into the dish, stir the cream into the sauce and pour over the chicken.

Serve with rice or green pasta, salad or broccoli.

Tournedos Rossini

RECIPE

For the Espagnole sauce
1 oz (25 g) butter
1 carrot (peeled and diced)
1 onion (peeled and chopped)
2 rashers streaky bacon (de-rinded and chopped)
1 oz (25 g) plain flour
15 fl oz (450 ml) beef stock
1 bouquet garni

2 tbs (30 ml) tomato purée
salt and black pepper
For the tournedos
4 tournedos beef
4 slices white bread
2 oz (75 g) unsalted butter
4 tbs (60 ml) Madeira or Marsala
salt and black pepper

METHOD

Melt the butter, add the vegetables and bacon and cook for 10 minutes. Stir in the flour and cook for 3–4 minutes or until brown. Blend in the stock, stirring until the sauce has thickened. Add the bouquet garni, tomato purée and seasoning. Cover and simmer for 30 minutes. Strain through a sieve. Trim the tournedos and tie neatly. Cut 4 circles from the bread to fit the tournedos. Heat 1 oz (25 g) of the butter and fry the bread on both sides until golden and crisp. Drain on kitchen paper and keep warm.

Heat 1 oz (25 g) of the butter and fry the tournedos over a high heat for 2 minutes on each side. Remove and keep warm. Add the Madeira or Marsala to the pan and heat for a minute. Stir in the sauce and simmer for 5–10 minutes or until thick.

To serve, arrange the bread on a warmed dish, and place a tournedos on each. Pour a little sauce over each and serve the rest in a warmed sauce boat.
Serves 4.

MICHAEL HESELTINE

ENGELBERT
HUMPERDINCK

Steak & Onions

RECIPE

2 tbs (30 ml) oil
4 beef steaks
3 large onions (peeled and chopped)
8 oz (225 g) mushrooms
3 tomatoes (peeled and halved)
1 tbs (15 ml) tomato purée
2 tsp (10 ml) gravy powder, eg Bisto, mixed with ¼ pt (150 ml) water
mixed herbs to taste
Worcestershire sauce to taste

METHOD

Heat the oil and fry the steak and onions together until golden-brown. Transfer to an ovenproof dish, add all other ingredients and cook at Gas Mark 4 or 350°F/180°C for $1\frac{1}{4}$–$1\frac{1}{2}$ hours or until the meat is tender. *Serves 4.*

Derek's Hot Tip

RECIPE

1 lb (450 g) lean minced beef
1 medium onion (peeled and finely chopped)
2 beef stock cubes
14 oz (400 g) tin tomatoes
1 tsp (5 ml) salt
2 tsp (10 ml) chilli powder
14 oz (400 g) tin red kidney beans
2 tsp (10 ml) dried mixed herbs
1 tsp (5 ml) ground mixed spice
4 oz (100 g) tin sliced mushrooms
1 tsp (5 ml) gravy browning

METHOD

Brown mince on low heat in a large saucepan, then add enough boiling water to cover meat. Add the onion, stock cubes and tomatoes, removing stalks and skin. Stir into meat and simmer for 15 minutes. Add salt, chilli powder, mixed herbs, mixed spice and gravy browning. Simmer for at least 20 minutes until sauce is thick. Stir in kidney beans and mushrooms, simmer for another 5 minutes and serve.

Tastes best with plain rice or baked potatoes. *Serves 3–4.*

DEREK
JAMESON

JOHN KETTLEY

Chilli Con Carne

RECIPE

2 tbs (30 ml) oil
1 large onion (peeled and sliced)
2 cloves garlic (peeled and crushed)
1 tsp (5 ml) crushed dried chilli or chilli powder
¾ lb (350 g) lean minced beef
14 oz (400 g) tin red kidney beans
2 tsp (10 ml) Worcestershire sauce
4 tbs (60 ml) tomato ketchup
¼ pt (150 ml) water
salt and pepper

METHOD

Heat the oil and fry the onion for 5 minutes or until golden-brown. Stir in the garlic, chilli powder and beef and cook over a moderate heat for 10 minutes.

Stir in all remaining ingredients and simmer for a further 30–35 minutes, adding more water if necessary.

Serve with boiled rice, allowing 3 oz per person. *Serves 4.*

Steak au Poivre

RECIPE

1 entrecôte (sirloin) or rump steak, weighing 6–8 oz (175–225 g)
2 tsp (10 ml) Dijon mustard
2 tsp (10 ml) whole black peppercorns
1 clove garlic (peeled and crushed – optional)
1 oz (25 g) butter

METHOD

Spread a thin layer of Dijon mustard on both sides of the steak. Crush black peppercorns, and the garlic if desired, and put on both sides of the steak.

Melt the butter in a pan and, when hot, sizzle the steak for 2–3 minutes each side, depending on the thickness of the steak, and how you like it cooked.

Once the steak is cooked, you can use the juices in the pan as a sauce. *Serves 1.*

RICHARD KEYS

"I enjoy hot, spicy food, and so this is how I would prepare this dish. However, if you don't like your food too spicy, don't use too many peppercorns!"

SUE LAWLEY

"Everyone will believe you have gone to an enormous amount of trouble to create a very rich and spicy chicken casserole."

Spicy Chicken

RECIPE

4 lb (1·8 kg) chicken
1¼ pt (750 ml) double cream
5 tbs (75 ml) white sauce
2 tbs (30 ml) mushroom ketchup
2 tsp (10 ml) made English mustard
salt and pepper

METHOD

Place the chicken in a roasting tin, and cover with buttered foil. Roast for 1¼–1½ hours at Gas Mark 6 or 400°F/200°C, or until cooked. (Pierce the thickest part of the thigh with a skewer – the juices should be golden and clear.) Allow the chicken to cool, then skin and cut into joints.

Mix together all remaining ingredients. Place the chicken joints in a shallow ovenproof dish. Thickly spread the cream mixture over and bake at Gas Mark 7 or 425°F/220°C for 20–25 minutes. *Serves 4.*

Chicken & Broccoli Bake

RECIPE

2 chickens [approx 3 lb (1·5 kg) each]
1 lb (450 g) broccoli
2 × 10 oz (275 g) tins Campbells condensed mushroom soup
1 tsp (5 ml) mild curry powder
3 tbs (45 ml) mayonnaise

6 oz (175 g) grated Cheddar cheese
6 oz (175 g) breadcrumbs
½ oz (10 g) butter
salt and black pepper
½ lb (225 g) mushrooms (sliced)
½ pt (300 ml) double cream

METHOD

Roast the chickens at Gas Mark 6 or 400°F/200°C for $1\frac{1}{4}$–$1\frac{1}{2}$ hours, or until cooked. Allow to cool, then carve all meat and place in the bottom of a large casserole. Cut the broccoli into smaller pieces, cook for 2 minutes in boiling water, drain thoroughly, then place on top of the chicken. Melt the butter and gently fry the mushrooms until soft. Sprinkle with salt and pepper. Mix together the mushroom soup, double cream, mayonnaise and curry powder, then pour on top of the other ingredients. Mix together the breadcrumbs and the grated cheese and sprinkle evenly on top of the casserole.

Place uncovered in the middle of the oven and cook at Gas Mark 4 or 350°F/180°C for 45–50 minutes or until heated through and the cheese and breadcrumb topping has become crisp. *Serves 6.*

MAUREEN LIPMAN

"This would be what I would make were I to host a dinner party for the 549 people to whom I owe dinner and that's just in London and the home counties! I comfort myself with the fact that I'm a perfect guest."

NIGEL
MANSELL

Normandy Chicken

RECIPE

1 tbs (15 ml) oil
4 oz (100 g) butter
3 lb (1·5 kg) chicken, cut into portions
2 shallots (finely chopped)
1 oz (25 g) flour
¾ pt (450 ml) dry cider

4 fl oz (120 ml) chicken stock
1 tsp (5 ml) dried mixed herbs
salt and freshly ground black pepper
1 lb (450 g) dessert apples (peeled, cored and
thickly sliced)
2 tbs (30 ml) Calvados (optional)

METHOD

Heat the oil and half the butter in a frying pan and fry the chicken portions until golden brown all over. Remove the chicken portions from the pan and transfer to a casserole. Fry the shallots in the fat remaining in the pan, then sprinkle in the flour and cook, stirring constantly, until light brown. Gradually stir in the cider, stock and herbs and bring to the boil, stirring constantly. Cook until the sauce has thickened, season to taste and pour over the chicken.

Cover the casserole and cook at Gas Mark 4 or 350°F/180°C for 1 hour, or until the chicken is just tender. Meanwhile, melt the remaining butter in a pan and cook the apple slices for about 2 minutes, stirring occasionally, until golden brown. Add the Calvados, if using, and spoon the apples on top of the chicken. *Serves 4–6.*

Rognons Sauté au Vin Rouge

RECIPE

3 or 4 lambs' kidneys
1 oz (25 g) butter
1 small onion (peeled and finely chopped)
4 oz (100 g) mushrooms (wiped and sliced)
salt and pepper
½ pt (300 ml) red wine
2 tbs (30 ml) chopped fresh parsley

METHOD

Skin and clean the kidneys and cut into slices. Melt the butter, add the onion and sauté for 3 minutes. Add the mushrooms – preferably use flat mushrooms, as they have more flavour – season the kidneys with salt and pepper and add to the pan. Cook for about 5 minutes, shaking the pan from time to time.

Pour the wine into the pan and simmer for 2 minutes. Remove the kidneys and vegetables with a slotted spoon and place on a warmed serving dish. Boil the remaining liquid until it has reduced to a thick sauce. Pour the sauce over the kidneys, sprinkle with parsley and serve immediately. *Serves 2.*

FRANCIS MATTHEWS

"As an ancient Yorkshireman my honest choice would have been a hearty roast beef and Yorkshire pudding (as a starter on its own – in gravy!) followed by roly-poly or spotted dick. But you have to be exotic in this kind of book and show off a bit!"

SIMON MAYO

Chicken Delight

RECIPE

3 lb (1·5 kg) cooked chicken (cut into thin strips)
2 oz (50 g) butter
1 onion (sliced)
4 oz (100 g) mushrooms (sliced)
2 oz (50 g) plain flour
1 pt (600 ml) milk
1 ½ tsp (7·5 ml) French mustard
salt and pepper
a small bag crisps (crushed)
3 oz (75 g) Cheddar cheese (grated)

METHOD

Melt the butter in a saucepan, add the onions and mushrooms and cook for 5 minutes. Stir in the flour, then gradually add the milk. Bring to the boil and simmer for 2–3 minutes. Stir in the mustard and seasoning. Add the chicken to the sauce and mix well. Spoon the mixture into a heatproof dish, sprinkle crisps and cheese over the top and cook under a grill for 4–5 minutes or until golden brown. *Serves 6.*

Spaghetti Bolognese Sauce

RECIPE

1 lb (450 g) minced beef
1 large onion (peeled and chopped)
1 clove garlic (peeled and crushed)
2 tbs (30 ml) oil, ½ oz (10 g) butter
1½ lb (675 g) tomatoes (skinned and chopped)
2 oz (50 g) tin tomato purée
shake of marjoram and thyme

1 green pepper (de-seeded and chopped)
4 oz (100 g) mushrooms (wiped and sliced)
2 sticks celery (sliced)
1 carrot (peeled and sliced)
1 bay leaf, salt and pepper
¼ pt (150 ml) wine
¼ pt (150 ml) beef stock

METHOD

Heat the oil and butter, add the garlic and onion and sauté for 5 minutes. Add the mince and cook until the meat is brown. Add the tomatoes, pepper, celery, carrots and mushrooms. Stir in the purée, bay leaf and herbs. Add the wine, stock, salt and pepper. Bring to the boil and simmer uncovered for 40–45 minutes or until thick. Serve with spaghetti and Parmesan cheese.

Whatever the weather, there's nothing like a satisfying meal to make the outlook brighter.

JULIA MCKENZIE

Creamy Smoked Salmon Pâté

RECIPE

8 oz (225 g) smoked salmon pieces
8 oz (225 g) cream cheese
2 tbs (30 ml) lemon juice
2 tbs (30 ml) single cream or top of the milk
pepper
1 lemon (cut into wedges)

METHOD

Grind the smoked salmon and combine thoroughly with the cream cheese, lemon juice, cream or top of the milk and pepper. Refrigerate for at least 1 hour before serving with hot toast and lemon wedges.
Serves 4.

Chicken Indienne

RECIPE

8 oz (225 g) cooked chicken
1 green pepper (de-seeded and sliced)
1 red pepper (de-seeded and sliced)
For the dressing
grated rind and juice ½ lemon
4 tbs (60 ml) mayonnaise
salt and pepper

METHOD

Cut the chicken into strips about $\frac{1}{4}$ in (1 cm) thick and 1 in (2·5 cm) wide. Place in a bowl with the pepper slices and mix well.

To make the dressing: mix together the lemon rind, juice and mayonnaise and season with salt and pepper. Pour over the chicken mixture and toss together. Garnish with slices of lemon before serving.
Serves 3–4.

MIKE MORRIS

"Don't ask me to cook it – I'm a disaster at anything more sophisticated than spaghetti bolognese or an omelette! It's ideal for summer – although I could eat it at any time."

JOHN NETTLES

"I discovered this traditional Jersey recipe while living over here on the island. It is a simple dish which even I can prepare with ease. Best eaten after a long day at sea or in the fields and washed down with a bottle of fruity beaujolais (or two)."

Un Piot et des Pois au Fou

RECIPE

4 oz (100 g) dried butter beans
4 oz (100 g) dried large red haricot beans
4 oz (100 g) dried brown beans
4 oz (100 g) dried small pearl haricot beans
2 lb (900 g) belly pork or 2 pigs trotters
4 oz (100 g) fresh broad beans
seasoning, herbs

METHOD

Soak the dried beans overnight, drain and place in a large pan with the meat and cover with water. Add the seasoning. Bring to the boil and simmer for 30 minutes. Skim, then pour into a casserole, adding fresh broad beans and herbs to your liking. Cover and bake at Gas Mark 2–3 or 300° – 325°F/150°–170°C for 4 hours.

Lambs' Kidneys

in Butter & Mustard Sauce

RECIPE

6 lambs' kidneys
1 oz (25 g) butter
1 tbs (15 ml) spring or ordinary onions (finely chopped)
4 fl oz (100 ml) dry white wine
1 tbs (15 ml) Dijon mustard
salt, pepper
2 tbs (30 ml) chopped parsley

METHOD

Remove the outer fat and skin from the kidneys. Melt the butter in a shallow casserole or deep frying pan. Add the kidneys and cook on both sides for about 10 minutes then move to a warm plate. Add the onions to the pan and cook for 1 minute. Add the white wine and boil while scraping up the bits on the bottom of the pan. Remove from heat. Add the mustard, salt and pepper to taste.

Slice the kidneys and add to the casserole. Put on a low heat for a couple of minutes to heat the kidneys through.

Sprinkle parsley on top and serve with boiled rice. *Serves 2.*

DAVID OWEN

93

CECIL
PARKINSON

Lancashire Hot Pot

RECIPE

2 tbs (30 ml) oil
2 lb (900 g) best end of neck chops
2 large onions (peeled and chopped)
4 large potatoes (peeled and sliced)
1 pt (600 ml) beef stock
salt and pepper

METHOD

Heat the oil in a frying pan and cook the meat until browned. Remove from the pan. Place a layer of meat in the bottom of a heavy casserole dish, then a layer of onions, then a layer of potatoes. Add the beef stock, salt and pepper. Finish with a layer of potato, completely covering the top. Cover and simmer over a low heat for 2 hours, until the meat is tender. Before serving, place under a hot grill to brown and crisp the top layer of potatoes. *Serves 4.*

Turkey & Cider Gougère

RECIPE

For the choux pastry
¼ pt (150 ml) water
2 oz (50 g) butter
2½ oz (60 g) plain flour
2 eggs (size 3)
For the filling
3 oz (75 g) butter
1 onion (chopped)

1½ oz (40 g) plain flour
¼ pt (150 ml) milk
¼ pt (150 ml) cider
salt and pepper
8 oz (225 g) cooked, diced turkey
7 oz (200 g) tin sweetcorn (drained)
1 tbs (15 ml) chopped parsley
6 oz (175 g) button mushrooms

METHOD

To prepare the choux pastry: heat the water and butter in a saucepan and bring to the boil. Remove from the heat, and add the flour all at once. Beat until the mixture leaves the sides of the saucepan. Allow to cool slightly. Beat in the eggs, one at a time, until you have a glossy paste. Put the mixture into a piping bag with a 1 in (2·5 cm) plain nozzle, and put to one side while you prepare the filling. Melt the butter in a pan. Fry the onion gently until tender. Stir in the flour and cook for 1 minute. Remove from the heat and gradually add the milk and cider. Bring to the boil, season, and stir in the cooked turkey, corn, parsley and mushrooms. Heat through and spoon the mixture in the centre of a greased 2 pt (1·2 l) ovenproof dish. Pipe the choux pastry around the turkey and cook at Gas Mark 5 or 375°F/190°C for 30–35 minutes. Serve straight from the oven. *Serves 4.*

GEOFFREY PEARCE

Commodore of the International Yachting Fellowship of Rotarians of Great Britain

"This tasty dish was 'invented' by our eldest daughter when she took her 'O' level cookery – for which she got an A grade."

MARJORIE PROOPS

"The beauty of this dish is that you can leave it for much longer on a very low heat so it's a good one for working wives. I serve my meatballs on plain, boiled, fluffy rice. It's a great standby, especially if you've got a mob of hungry teenagers to feed."

Meatballs in Tomato Sauce

RECIPE

For the meatballs
1 tbs (15 ml) oil
1 lb (450 g) minced beef
4 oz (100 g) sausage meat
1 tsp (5 ml) mixed herbs
1 clove garlic (peeled and crushed – optional)
1 tbs (15 ml) chopped fresh parsley
1 medium onion (peeled and finely chopped)

1 egg, salt and pepper
For the tomato sauce
1 tbs (15 ml) oil
1 onion (peeled and chopped)
14 oz (400 g) tin tomatoes
2 tbs (30 ml) tomato purée
½ pt (300 ml) beef stock
salt and pepper

METHOD

To make the meatballs: mix all the ingredients except the oil together. With floured hands, roll into walnut-sized balls. Flatten the balls and put on to a floured board. Fry them quickly in hot oil for 2–3 minutes. Drain on kitchen paper and put into a casserole. Meanwhile, make the tomato sauce: heat the oil and fry the onion. Add the tomatoes, tomato purée, stock, salt and pepper. Let this bubble for a few moments and then pour it over the meatballs in the casserole. Place the lid on the casserole and put on the middle shelf of the oven at Gas Mark 3 or 325°F/170°C for $2\frac{1}{2}$ hours. *Serves 4–6.*

Cottage Pie

RECIPE

2½ lb (1·1 kg) lean minced beef
1 lb (450 g) onions (peeled and sliced)
3 tbs (45 ml) sunflower oil
2 oz (50 g) flour
8 oz (225 g) tomato purée
7 fl oz (200 ml) red wine
10 fl oz (300 ml) stock

black pepper, salt
1 bouquet garni
3½ lb (1·5 kg) potatoes
butter
milk
3 oz (75 g) cheese (grated)

METHOD

Heat the oil and sauté the onions until tender. Add the meat and continue cooking, stirring with a wooden spoon. Stir in the flour and tomato purée and mix well. Add the wine, stock, salt, pepper and bouquet garni and simmer for 2 hours. Remove the bouquet garni.

Boil the potatoes until tender, mash with the milk and butter to taste, then fork on top of the mince. Sprinkle the cheese on top and bake at Gas Mark 6 or 400°F/200°C for 30 minutes or until the top is golden brown. *Serves 8.*

PETER DE SAVARY

"I enjoy plain English food more than any other."

PHILLIP
SCHOFIELD

"This is a really quick recipe to do and, if you halve the ingredients, it is perfect for an evening for two."

Grilled Trout with Orange & Almonds

RECIPE

4 trout (cleaned)
2 oz (50 g) butter
4 oz (100 g) flaked almonds
juice of 2 oranges
salt and pepper

METHOD

Sprinkle the trout with salt and pepper. Pre-heat the grill and cook the trout under a high heat for 5–6 minutes on each side until golden brown. Melt the butter, add the almonds and orange juice and cook until the almonds begin to colour. Pour over the grilled trout before serving. *Serves 4.*

Turkey Crunch

RECIPE

½ oz (10 g) butter
1 tbs (15 ml) oil
12 oz (350 g) turkey fillet (uncooked)
1 medium onion (finely chopped)
2 celery stalks (chopped)
14 oz (400 g) tin condensed mushroom soup
2 tbs (30 ml) mayonnaise
1 tbs (15 ml) lemon juice
pinch cayenne pepper
2 tbs (30 ml) parsley (chopped)
small packet potato crisps (plain)
3 hard boiled eggs
1 tomato (sliced)

METHOD

Brown the turkey, onions and celery in a frying pan with the oil and butter. Put in an ovenproof dish. Mix together the soup, mayonnaise, lemon juice, pepper and parsley and spoon over the turkey and vegetables. Crush the crisps and sprinkle on top. Cook at Gas Mark 4 or 350°F/180°C for 35–40 minutes. Garnish with eggs and tomato. Serve with green salad and new potatoes or rice. *Serves 4.*

DOREEN SLOANE

Annabelle Collins from *Brookside*

CYRIL SMITH

Hot Pot

RECIPE

2 tbs (30 ml) oil
1 lb (450 g) beef chuck steak cut into 1 in (2·5 cm) cubes
1 pt (600 ml) water
6 medium potatoes (peeled and sliced)
6 medium onions (peeled and sliced)
6 carrots (peeled and sliced)
1 tsp (5 ml) salt
1 lb (450 g) can tomatoes
½ tsp (2·5 ml) Tabasco sauce

METHOD

Heat the oil in a frying pan and cook the beef until well-browned. Remove. Add water to the fat in the pan. Cook, stirring constantly to blend the bits of meat left in the pan. Remove from the heat. Layer the beef, potatoes, onions and carrots in a casserole, sprinkling each layer with salt and a little Tabasco, and adding tomatoes on each layer. Finish with a layer of potato. Pour over the stock. Cook at Gas Mark 4 or 350°F/180°C for 2–2½ hours or until beef is very tender. *Serves 6.*

Kind Hearts & Coronets

RECIPE

For the coronets
5 large firm tomatoes
1 tsp (5 ml) caster sugar
1 tbs (15 ml) freshly chopped or 1 tsp (5 ml)
dried basil
salt and ground black pepper
For the stuffed hearts
4 large or 8 small lambs' hearts

2 oz (50 g) shredded suet
2 oz (50 g) bacon (diced)
4 oz (100 g) breadcrumbs
2 tsp (10 ml) chopped parsley
½ tsp (2·5 ml) mixed herbs
grated rind ½ lemon
1 egg (beaten)
salt and ground black pepper

METHOD

Using a small sharp knife, make a series of small V-shaped cuts around the middle of each tomato. Carefully pull the two halves apart. Sprinkle with sugar, basil, salt and pepper. Leave in the fridge for at least one hour.

Wash the hearts and cut away gristle and tendons from the inside, to leave a cavity. Make the stuffing by mixing together all remaining ingredients, and spoon into the hearts.

Place the hearts in a greased baking tin and cook at Gas Mark 4 or 350°F/180°C for 1 hour or until cooked. Serve with the tomatoes, potato crisps, cos lettuce, radishes and raw onion rings. *Serves 4.*

RICHARD STILGOE

"There are five tomatoes because one of them is bound to go wrong."

VIVIEN STUART

"I enjoy this meal with a cooling side dish of yoghurt or tsatsiki. If you like it hot (some do!) 4 tbs of chilli powder will pack a punch."

Chilli Con Carne

RECIPE

8 oz (225 g) dried red kidney beans
2 tbs (30 ml) hot chilli powder
1 tsp (5 ml) salt
1 tsp (5 ml) each cayenne pepper, oregano and cumin,
2 bay leaves
1 × 14 oz (400 g) can tomatoes
3 oz (75 g) tomato purée
2/3 cloves garlic (crushed)
2 medium onions (peeled and chopped)
1½ lb (675 g) lean chuck steak (chopped into small cubes)
1 pt (600 ml) beef stock

METHOD

Cover the kidney beans with cold water, bring to the boil and boil rapidly for 10 minutes. Turn off the heat, cover, and let them soak for 20 minutes. Drain.

Place all the ingredients in a large casserole dish and cook at Gas Mark 4 or 350°F/180°C for $2\frac{1}{2}$–3 hours, stirring occasionally, until the beans are tender and the sauce is thick. Serve with boiled rice or garlic bread and a nice salad. *Serves 4–6.*

Chinese Lemon Chicken

RECIPE

3 chicken breasts
juice 1 lemon
3 tbs (45 ml) cornflour
3 tbs (45 ml) flour
salt and pepper
2 tbs (30 ml) oil
For the sauce
1 tbs (15 ml) each of tomato purée, soy sauce, wine vinegar, corn oil

METHOD

Place the chicken in a shallow glass dish. Pour lemon juice over, cover and marinate in the refrigerator for 1–2 hours. Mix the flour and cornflour together. Cut the chicken into 1 in (2.5 cm) cubes and coat with the flour mixture. Heat the oil in a wok or deep frying pan, until very hot, then quickly fry the chicken until golden brown and thoroughly cooked, turning constantly. Drain on kitchen paper and keep warm.

To make the sauce: mix together all ingredients. Pour into a wok and stir over a high heat for 30 seconds. Return the chicken to the wok, coat with sauce and serve immediately with rice and stir-fry vegetables. *Serves 4.*

DAVID SUCHET

"A favourite with all our family, I've chosen this because, apart from being quite delicious, whenever we have this dish our children dash away to dress up in Chinese dressing gowns and we all drink pots of jasmine tea and manage with chopsticks and bowls. It has become a special family event."

Lamb Romagna

RECIPE

1 tbs (15 ml) oil
1 medium onion (chopped)
2 oz (50 g) celery (chopped)
1 clove garlic (crushed)
4 lamb chops
salt and pepper
1 lb (450 g) courgettes
1 pt (600 ml) tomato juice
2 tbs (30 ml) fresh mint (chopped)

METHOD

Heat the oil in a large pan. Add the onion, celery and garlic to the pan and sauté until soft. Season the lamb chops with salt and pepper. Add to the pan and brown for 2 minutes on both sides. Transfer to a casserole dish. Slice the courgettes, and add to the dish with the tomato juice. Sprinkle with mint. Cook for approximately $1\frac{1}{4}$ hours, at Gas Mark 2 or 300°F/150°C. *Serves 4.*

Fresh Salmon Mousse

RECIPE

1 lb (450 g) fresh salmon
1 pt (600 ml) Court Bouillon or Knorr fish
stock
½ pt (300 ml) double cream (lightly whipped)
2 oz (50 g) butter (softened)

4 fl oz (100 ml) dry sherry
2 tbs (30 ml) lemon juice
salt and cayenne pepper
½ oz (10 g) powdered gelatine

METHOD

Set the oven to Gas Mark 4 or 350°F/180°C. Wipe the salmon with a damp cloth and put into a buttered ovenproof dish. Pour over hot Court Bouillon (or fish stock), cover with foil and cook in the oven for 20 minutes. Leave the salmon to cool in the liquid, then remove the skin and bones. Pound the salmon until smooth then fold in the cream. Stir in the softened butter, sherry and lemon juice and blend thoroughly. Season to taste. Put 6 tbs (90 ml) of hot Court Bouillon/fish stock into a bowl and sprinkle on the gelatine. Put the bowl over a saucepan of boiling water and stir the mixture until the gelatine has completely dissolved. Cool slightly and beat into the salmon mixture.

Spoon the mousse into a lightly oiled mould and leave to set for several hours or overnight in the fridge. Turn out on to a serving plate and garnish with lemon, cucumber, tomato and mayonnaise.

CHRIS TARRANT

Chris is an avid fisherman and makes this recipe with Court Bouillon – a sauce that goes well with any poached or boiled fish. "I usually serve this as a starter and add quartered slices of wholemeal bread or toast."

NORMAN TEBBIT

Beef Wellington

RECIPE

2 lb (900 g) fillet of beef
freshly ground black pepper
4 oz (100 g) button mushrooms (wiped)
2 tsp (10 ml) chopped mixed herbs and
parsley

1 oz (25 g) butter
8 oz (225 g) puff pastry
egg for glazing, watercress to garnish
½ lb (225 g) smooth pâté

METHOD

Trim and tie up the fillet. Melt half the butter and brush over the fillet, then sprinkle with black pepper. Place in a roasting tin and cook at Gas Mark 6 or 400°F/200°C for 15 minutes. Take out and allow to cool. Slice the mushrooms, sauté in remaining butter for 10 minutes or until all the moisture has evaporated. Add the herbs and cool. Roll out the puff pastry to a rectangle approximately 14 × 10 in (35·5 × 25·5 cm). Trim edges off pastry. Spread the mushroom mixture in the centre. Slice the meat in half lengthways and spread pâté on to the meat, then put the whole thing on to the mushroom mixture.

Brush the edges of the pastry with beaten egg and wrap the pastry around the meat like a parcel. Place join side down on a lightly greased baking sheet. Brush with egg to glaze, and decorate with "fleurons" made from the pastry trimmings. Bake at Gas Mark 8 or 450°F/230°C for 35–40 minutes, or until well browned. Serve hot or cold, garnished with watercress. *Serves 6.*

Molly's Mealy Pudding

RECIPE

6 oz (175 g) medium oatmeal
4 oz (100 g) suet or dripping
4 oz (100 g) minced beef (cooked)
2 oz (50 g) chopped cooked onions (fried in dripping)
1 tsp (5 ml) each of parsley and thyme
salt and freshly ground black pepper
gravy or vegetable stock to mix

METHOD

Mix all ingredients together to a soft mixture with the gravy or stock, but don't get it *too* sloppy, just wet enough to drop off a wooden spoon. Put it in to a 2–2½ pt (1·25–1·5 l) greased basin, cover with foil or greaseproof paper, tied down to stop water bubbling into the mixture. Place in a saucepan of water, bring to the boil and keep it topped up and boiling for 3 hours, just as for any other steamed pudding.

It doesn't spoil by being kept, and it can be re-heated the next day in your saucepan of water as before, again covered and tied down.

MOLLY WEIR

"The mealy pudding is very particular to Scotland and is really delicious, as a savoury stuffing or an 'extra' to eke out any sort of meat."

ALAN WHICKER

"Despite all the exotic places I visit, I like simple, plain food such as steak, fish and fruit."

Whicker's Chinese Chicken

RECIPE

2 tbs (30 ml) light soy sauce
1 tbs (15 ml) sherry
1 tbs (15 ml) cornflour
½ tsp (2·5 ml) each of sugar and salt
4 chicken breasts (cut into slices)
4 tbs (60 ml) oil
6 oz (175 g) celery (sliced)
6 oz (175 g) onions (peeled and chopped)
8 oz (225 g) peas (fresh or frozen)

1 red pepper (de-seeded and diced)
1 clove garlic (peeled and crushed)
½ in (1·5 cm) fresh ginger (peeled and finely grated)
7 oz (200 g) can whole button mushrooms (reserve liquid)
4 fl oz (100 ml) reserved mushroom liquid
4 oz (100 g) whole almonds

METHOD

Mix together the soy sauce, sherry, cornflour, sugar and salt. Add the chicken, stir and leave to stand for 15 minutes. Heat a wok, pour in 1 tbs (15 ml) of the oil and heat. Add the celery and onions and stir-fry for 1–2 minutes. Set aside. Add 1 tbs (15 ml) oil and stir-fry the peas with the red pepper for 1–2 minutes. Set aside. Add 2 tbs (30 ml) oil and cook the crushed garlic and ginger for 1 minute. Add the chicken and cook for 3–4 minutes until lightly browned. Stir in the button mushrooms, mushroom liquid and almonds. Return the reserved vegetables to the pan and simmer until the sauce has reduced and thickened. Serve immediately. *Serves 4.*

Rich Fruit Cake

RECIPE

2 oz (50 g) treacle	½ tsp (2.5 ml) mixed spice
8 oz (225 g) butter or margarine	½ tsp (2.5 ml) almond essence
6 oz (150 g) caster sugar	grated rind of 1 lemon or orange
4 eggs, pinch salt	2 lb (900 g) mixed dried fruit
12 oz (350 g) flour	4 oz (100 g) candied peel
¼ tsp (1 ml) baking powder	4 oz (100 g) glacé cherries
pinch grated nutmeg	1 tbs (15 ml) milk
pinch ground cinnamon	8 in (20 cm) round cake tin

METHOD

Grease the tin and line with greased paper, which stands up above the tin. Cut a circle to fit the base, then tie brown paper doubled round the outside of the tin. Soften the treacle in a teacup standing in warm water. Cream the sugar and butter or margarine. Add the treacle and mix well. Beat the eggs, then add slowly to the mixture, beating well after each addition. Sift the flour, salt, baking powder, nutmeg, cinnamon and mixed spice. Fold into the mixture with the fruit, almond essence and rind. Add the milk if necessary for a soft dropping consistency. Turn into the tin, and top with greased greaseproof paper on top.

Bake at Gas Mark 4 or 350°F/180°C for 1 hour. Remove paper from the top, then lower the oven to Gas Mark 2 or 300°F/150°C. Bake for a further 2 to 2½ hours, or until a skewer comes out clean. When cool, ice the cake, if liked.

**PETER MURRAY
(COXSWAIN)
ANSTRUTHER STATION,
SCOTLAND
(Oakley Class)
'THE DOCTORS'**

RUSS ABBOT

Although Russ does not cook himself, he is very fond of this recipe, especially when it is served with custard and a dollop of vanilla ice cream

Gooseberry Pie

RECIPE

8 oz (225 g) plain flour
pinch salt
2 oz (50 g) butter or margarine
2 oz (50 g) lard
cold water to mix

1½ lb (675 g) gooseberries (topped and tailed)
4 oz (100 g) caster sugar
finely grated rind ½ orange
1 tbs (15 ml) milk

METHOD

Sift the flour and salt into a bowl. Add the butter or margarine and lard, cut into pieces, and rub in until the mixture resembles breadcrumbs. Stir in enough water to make a soft dough. Wrap and chill for 20 minutes.

Roll out a little more than half of the pastry and line a 9½ in (24 cm) pie dish. Dampen the edge with water. Mix together the gooseberries, sugar and orange rind and spoon into the pastry case.

Roll out remaining pastry to a circle the size of the pie dish and place over the filling, pressing firmly to seal. Trim and flute the edge and make an air vent in the centre.

Brush the top of the pie with milk and bake at Gas Mark 6 or 400°F/200°C for 45 minutes, or until the pastry is golden brown and the gooseberries tender when pierced with a skewer. Serve warm with custard or ice cream. *Serves 6.*

Baked Stuffed Peaches

RECIPE

4 large firm peaches (halved, skinned and stoned)
1 oz (25 g) butter
2 oz (50 g) soft brown sugar
2 oz (50 g) ground almonds
4 cocktail sticks
4 tbs (60 ml) rum
brown sugar for sprinkling

METHOD

Mix the butter, 1 oz (25g) soft brown sugar and almonds. Spoon mixture into the 4 peach halves, place the other halves on top and hold in place with the cocktail sticks. Place in a buttered dish, close together, and sprinkle with remaining brown sugar and rum.

Bake at Gas Mark 4 or 350°F/180°C for 15–20 minutes, basting occasionally to prevent peaches drying out. Serve immediately with whipped cream. *Serves 4.*

PETER ALLISS

"With the peaches being fresh, I kid myself it's a slimming pud!"

111

RONNIE
BARKER

Grape Special

RECIPE

1 lb (450 g) seedless grapes (if unavailable, de-pipping is essential)
½ pt (300 ml) double cream
large block vanilla ice cream
4 oz (100 g) soft brown sugar

METHOD

Put the grapes into a fireproof dish, cover with the cream, and put into a fridge overnight. About 10 or 12 minutes before the dish is required, light the grill. Cover the grapes and cream with thick slices of ice cream, then cover ice cream with at least a $\frac{1}{4}$ in (5 mm) of brown sugar, making sure no ice cream is showing through. Put under a very hot grill until the surface of the sugar is sizzling. A few seconds after removing from the grill, the sugar will cool and form a toffee apple-type surface over the whole dish. *Serves 4.*

Oat Biscuits

RECIPE

4 oz (100 g) self-raising flour
3 oz (75g) fats (mixture of butter, margarine and lard is ideal)
3 oz (75 g) Quaker oats
1 oz (25 g) caster sugar
pinch of salt
1 tbs (15 ml) milk

METHOD

Mix together the flour and salt. Rub in the fat then stir in the oats and sugar and mix to a stiff paste with the milk.

Roll out thinly on a floured board and cut into rounds. Bake on a greased baking sheet for 15–20 minutes, at Gas Mark 4 or 350°F/180°C.

SIR RHODES BOYSON

MELVYN
BRAGG

Bread & Butter Pudding

RECIPE

½ pt (300 ml) milk
2 oz (50 g) caster sugar
3 eggs
8 slices of bread
2 oz (50 g) currants
ground nutmeg
butter

METHOD

Butter the bread, cut the slices in half and place one layer of bread over the base of a buttered dish. Sprinkle over half the currants. Cover with the remaining bread and currants.

Whisk together the sugar, eggs and milk. Pour over the bread and sprinkle with ground nutmeg. Bake for 30–40 minutes at Gas Mark 4 or 350°F/180°C. *Serves 4–6.*

Bread & Butter Pudding

RECIPE

3 slices brown bread (with crusts removed)
1 oz (25 g) butter
2 tbs (30 ml) sultanas (soaked in brandy – optional)
1 tbs (15 ml) sugar
2 eggs (lightly beaten)
¼ pt (150 ml) milk
¼ pt (150 ml) single cream
few drops vanilla essence
sprinkle ground cinnamon
1 tbs (15 ml) icing sugar

METHOD

Butter a shallow ovenproof dish. Butter the bread and cut into triangles. Sprinkle a few sultanas on the bottom of the dish, then arrange the bread, slightly overlapping, in the dish. Sprinkle on the remaining sultanas.

Mix the eggs, milk, cream, sugar and vanilla, then pour over the bread. Sprinkle a little cinnamon on the top. Leave to soak for at least half an hour.

Cook for 40 mins at Gas Mark 4 or 350°F/180°C. Dust with icing sugar and serve immediately. *Serves 4.*

RICHARD BRANSON

115

BILL
BUCKLEY

"This recipe was given to me by a very jolly vicar friend. He served it up at a dinner party and we all agreed it was the scrummiest pudding we'd ever eaten. Don't be put off by the bread among the ingredients — it really is a delight."

Cinders & Cream

RECIPE

4 oz (100 g) fresh brown breadcrumbs
4½ oz (125 g) demerara sugar
8 tbs (120 ml) drinking chocolate powder
2 tbs (30 ml) fine coffee powder
¼ pt (150 ml) single cream
½ pt (300 ml) double cream
2 oz (50 g) plain chocolate (grated)
1½ pt (900 ml) glass serving bowl

METHOD

Mix together the breadcrumbs, sugar, drinking chocolate and coffee powder. Mix together the single and double cream. Pour a third of the cream over the bottom of the dish and sprinkle half the dry mixture over. Top with a second layer of cream and dry mixture and finish with remaining cream. Press down firmly, then sprinkle grated chocolate on the top. Leave for 24 hours in the fridge or at least overnight, for the layers to soak up the flavours. *Serves 4–6.*

Christmas Pudding

RECIPE

6 oz (175 g) currants
6 oz (175 g) sultanas
12 oz (350 g) raisins
3 oz (75 g) mixed peel (chopped)
4 oz (100 g) flour
8 oz (225 g) breadcrumbs
8 oz (225 g) suet

8 oz (225 g) brown sugar
½ tsp (2.5 ml) mixed spice
1 oz (25 g) ground almonds
finely grated rind of 1 lemon
4 eggs (lightly beaten)
brandy, old ale or milk
pinch grated nutmeg

METHOD

Wash and pick over currants, sultanas and raisins. Put all the ingredients into a bowl, mix thoroughly with eggs and enough brandy, ale or milk to moisten the mixture. Leave mixture to soak overnight. Spoon into a well-buttered basin, cover with buttered paper and tie with string. Steam over boiling water for 8–9 hours. When cooled, store in a cool dry place until needed. Heat through by steaming for 2 hours. Makes two 2 pt (1 l) or four 1 pt (570 ml) puddings.

HARRY
CARPENTER

THE LATE
MAURICE
COLBOURNE

"This is a most refreshing dessert –
aromatic and rich tasting, but
leaves the palate feeling fresh at
the end of a meal. It is also simple
to do – just leave a little time to
de-pod the cardamoms and crush
them."

Cardamom Ice Cream

RECIPE

2 scoops vanilla ice cream
10 green cardamom pods
¼ oz (5 g) butter
1 banana
2 tbs (30 ml) single cream

METHOD

Peel the outer husks from the cardamom pods and remove the tiny
black seeds. Crush the seeds with a pestle and mortar. (Do not use
powdered cardamom bought from the shop.) Melt the butter in a
saucepan, add the crushed cardamom seeds and cook for 3–4 minutes
on a low heat. Peel and slice bananas. Add to the pan and cook for 1–
2 minutes. Stir in cream and bring to the boil. Remove from heat and
pour over individual servings of ice cream. *Serves 1.*

Chocolate Ice Cream Pie

RECIPE

8 oz (225 g) plain chocolate wheatmeal biscuits (crushed to crumbs)
2 oz (50 g) butter
1¾ pt (1 l) vanilla ice cream
2 oz (50 g) bitter chocolate (grated)

METHOD

Put the crushed biscuits into a mixing bowl. Heat the butter gently in a small saucepan and mix into the crumbs. Press the mixture into the base and sides of a $9\frac{1}{2}$ in (24 cm) tin. Bake at Gas Mark 5 or 375°F/190°C for 10 minutes. After, remove it and leave to get completely cold.

Empty the ice cream into a bowl and whisk it to soften slightly until it has a spreading consistency (do not let it melt completely). Spread half the ice cream in the biscuit-lined tin and sprinkle half the chocolate over the surface. Now spread the remaining ice cream and finish off with the rest of the chocolate on top. Cover the pie with foil or clingfilm and freeze for at least $1\frac{1}{2}$ hours before serving.

PHIL
COLLINS

EDWINA CURRIE

Carrot Cake

RECIPE

2 eggs (separated)
8 oz (225 g) soft brown sugar
6 oz (175 g) sunflower margarine (melted)
2 tbs (30ml) warm water
5 oz (150 g) wholemeal flour
1 tsp (5 ml) baking powder
½ tsp (2.5 ml) mixed spice
pinch salt
1 oz (25 g) walnuts, chopped

1 oz (25 g) sultanas
6 oz (175 g) carrots, grated
For the icing
4 oz (100 g) low fat soft cheese
4 oz (100 g) icing sugar (sifted)
rind of ½ lemon
2 lb (900 g) loaf tin or 7 in (18 cm) cake tin
(based, lined and greased)

METHOD

Cream together the egg yolks, sugar, margarine and water. Sieve the flour, baking powder, spice and salt into a bowl, add the nuts, sultanas and carrots, and mix. Make a well in the centre and add the egg mixture. Stir and mix thoroughly. Whisk the egg whites until standing in soft peaks. Fold carefully into the cake mixture.

Pour into the tin and bake at Gas Mark 5 or 375°F/190°C for 45–50 minutes, until a skewer inserted in the centre of the cake comes out clean. Cool on a wire rack.

To make the icing: cream together the soft cheese, and icing sugar, until soft and creamy. Add the lemon rind and swirl over the cake. Decorate with a little lemon rind.

Torta di Noci

RECIPE

6 oz (175 g) walnuts
6 oz (175 g) caster sugar
6 oz (175 g) chocolate (grated)
1 oz (25 g) candied peel (optional)
4 eggs (separated)
vanilla essence
1 oz (25 g) fine white breadcrumbs

METHOD

Pound the nuts and sugar in a pestle and mortar, until the nuts are ground. Mix with the chocolate, egg yolks and vanilla essence. Whisk the egg whites until stiff and fold in with the candied peel. Butter an 8 in (20 cm) pie dish and sprinkle the base with breadcrumbs. Spoon in the mixture and bake for 30 minutes at Gas Mark 4 or 350°F/180°C.
Serves 4.

PAUL EDDINGTON

"Eat at your peril – this dish is bad for you! I prefer to make it without the candied peel."

EDDIE
EDWARDS

Apple Pie

RECIPE

For the pastry
8 oz (225 g) plain flour
pinch salt
2 tbs (30 ml) icing sugar
4 oz butter or margarine
1 egg (beaten)
cold water to mix

For the filling
1½ lb (675 g) cooking apples
4 oz (100 g) soft brown sugar
1 tbs (15 ml) cornflour
½ tsp (2.5 ml) ground cinnamon
½ oz (10 g) butter
1 tbs (15 ml) icing or caster sugar

METHOD

Sift the flour, salt and icing sugar into a mixing bowl. Rub in the butter or margarine until the mixture resembles breadcrumbs. Stir in the egg and enough water to mix to a dough. Wrap and chill for 20 minutes. Meanwhile, peel, core and slice the apples. Mix together the sugar, cornflour and cinnamon. Sprinkle over the apples and mix well. Divide the pastry in two, one slightly larger than the other. Roll out the larger half to a circle large enough to line a 9 in (23 cm) shallow pie plate. Spoon in the sliced apples, adding a few dots of butter. Dampen the pastry rim. Roll remaining pastry and use to cover the top. Press the edges together firmly, and trim. Bake above the centre of the oven at Gas Mark 6 or 400°F/200°C for 40–45 minutes or until the pastry is brown and crisp. Dust with sugar and serve. *Serves 4–6.*

Cheese Scones

RECIPE

6 oz (175 g) self raising flour
1 oz (25 g) butter
4 oz (100 g) Cheddar cheese (grated)
1 large egg
pinch salt
¼ tsp (1 ml) cayenne pepper
¼ tsp (1 ml) dried mustard
3 tbs (45 ml) milk

METHOD

Mix the flour, salt and spices together. Rub in the butter. Add the grated cheese and bind with beaten egg and milk.

Roll out on a floured board to $\frac{1}{4}$ in (6 mm) thickness. Cut into rounds with a scone cutter.

Bake at Gas Mark 8 or 450°F/230°C in the middle of the oven for 10 minutes or until golden brown.

BRYAN FERRY

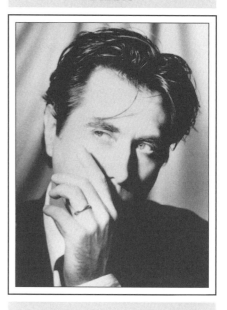

Bryan's mother provided this favourite recipe of his – she makes them for him when he comes home.

HANNAH
GORDON

"This is lovely sliced and buttered.
And it's a good recipe for children
because it's so nice and simple. I
usually use 81 per cent wholemeal
self raising flour."

Malt Loaf

RECIPE

10 oz (275 g) self raising flour
6 oz (175 g) dried mixed fruit
8 oz (225 g) dark soft brown sugar
1 tbs (15 ml) black treacle, dissolved in 8 fl oz (225 ml) warm milk
pinch salt

METHOD

Sieve together the flour and salt. Add all other ingredients and mix
with a metal spoon. Put the mixture in to a 1 lb (450 g) greased loaf
tin. Bake for 1 hour at Gas Mark 4 or 350°F/180°C. Leave in the tin
for a few minutes, then turn out and cool on a wire rack.

Toffee Nutty Bananas

SARAH
GREENE

RECIPE

1 oz (25 g) butter
2 tbs (30 ml) golden syrup
2 oz (50 g) soft brown sugar
2 tbs (30 ml) cream
2 bananas
2 large scoops vanilla ice cream
2 oz (50 g) walnuts or pecan nuts (chopped)

METHOD

Slowly melt the butter, syrup and sugar in a heavy saucepan, over a low heat. Be patient — it can take some time! When everything in the pan is completely melted, take the pan off the heat and slowly stir in the cream.

Cut up the bananas and arrange them in two dessert dishes. Plonk the ice cream over the top of the bananas in an arty way and pour the delicious sauce over the whole lot. Sprinkle walnuts or pecans over the sauce. Yummy! *Serves 2.*

"This is divine. I make it with variations of the recipe."

BOB
HOLNESS

Bob prefers this unusual topping
on his apple crumble.

Nutty Apple Crumble

RECIPE

1½ lb (675 g) cooking apples
1 oz (25 g) caster sugar
For the topping:
6 oz (175 g) plain flour
3 oz (75 g) butter or margarine
2 oz (50 g) caster sugar
1 oz (25 g) chopped mixed nuts
1 oz (25 g) sunflower seeds
2 oz (50 g) pecan nuts (chopped)

METHOD

Peel, core and slice the apples thinly. Place in a buttered 3-pt (1.7-l) pie dish, sprinkling the sugar between the layers.

For the topping: sift the flour into a mixing bowl, cut up the butter or margarine and rub in until the mixture resembles breadcrumbs. Stir in the caster sugar, chopped mixed nuts and sunflower seeds. Spoon this crumble mixture over the apples. Place the dish on a baking tray and bake on the centre shelf of the oven at Gas Mark 6 or 400°F/200°C for 40 minutes. Scatter the pecan nuts over the top and cook for a further 5 minutes.

Serve hot with custard or cream. *Serves 4.*

Crème Caramel

RECIPE

6 oz (175 g) caster sugar
5 fl oz (150 ml) single cream
5 fl oz (150 ml) milk
1 vanilla pod or few drops vanilla essence
3 eggs
2 egg yolks

METHOD

Place 4 oz (100 g) of the sugar in a heavy-based saucepan and heat. When the sugar melts and begins to darken stir and continue to cook until it is a light brown colour. Remove from the heat and carefully add 1 tbs (15 ml) hot water – the mixture will splutter. Pour into a $1\frac{1}{2}$ pt (900 ml) round baking dish.

Heat the cream and milk, with the vanilla pod or essence. Whisk together the remaining sugar, eggs and yolks. When the cream boils, pour over the egg mixture, stirring continuously. Remove the vanilla pod. Pour into a dish. Cook in a bain-marie (a pan of hot water) for 1 hour at Gas Mark 2 or 300°F/150°C. Cool and chill the crème caramel and turn out just before serving. *Serves 4–6.*

GLYN HOUSTON

FRANKIE
HOWERD

Nutty Chocolate Layer

RECIPE

1 packet chocolate blancmange mix
2 tbs (30 ml) caster sugar
1½ pt (900 ml) milk
2 chocolate Swiss rolls (sliced)
½ pt (300 ml) double cream
4 oz (100 g) mixed nuts (chopped)
3 pt (1.7 l) glass serving dish

METHOD

Make up the blancmange using the sugar and milk, following the packet instructions. Leave to cool for 5 minutes.

Arrange half the Swiss roll slices on the base and up the side of the serving dish. Pour in a third of the blancmange and top with a third of the remaining Swiss roll slices. Repeat layers ending with Swiss roll slices.

Whip the cream until thick and spoon over the top. Sprinkle with chopped nuts, and chill for at least 1 hour before serving. *Serves 6.*

Guards Pudding

BRIAN JOHNSTON

RECIPE

For the pudding
6 oz (175 g) fresh white breadcrumbs
6 oz (175 g) chopped shredded suet or butter
4 oz (100 g) soft brown sugar
3 tbs (45 ml) strawberry jam
1 large egg
1 level tsp (5 ml) bicarbonate of soda

pinch of salt
For the sauce
1 egg
1 egg yolk
1½ oz (30 g) caster sugar
2 tbs (30 ml) orange juice

METHOD

Mix together breadcrumbs, suet or butter and sugar. Stir together the jam, egg, bicarbonate of soda and salt. Add to the dry ingredients, mix thoroughly and then turn into a well-greased 2 pt (1 l) pudding basin. Cover the basin with a double piece of buttered foil, pleated in the middle, and tie with string. Steam over boiling water for 3 hours. Uncover, loosen the sides of the pudding with a palette knife, turn out onto a warm plate and serve hot.

Place all the ingredients for the sauce in a bowl over very hot water. Whisk until thick and frothy. Serve immediately. *Serves 4–6.*

KENNETH KENDALL

"This is a great favourite of mine and it is always popular with guests."

Quick Lemon Syllabub

RECIPE

½ pt (300 ml) double cream
2 lemons
2–4 oz (50–100 g) caster sugar
small glass sherry or brandy

METHOD

Beat together the cream and grated rind of one lemon. As it thickens, add the juice of both lemons and the sugar. Beat until soft peaks form. Taste, and add more lemon juice and sugar if necessary, then fold in the sherry or brandy. Serve in small glasses or pots. Chill for about an hour before serving. *Serves 4.*

Welsh Cakes

RECIPE

8 oz (225 g) self-raising flour
4 oz (100 g) butter or margarine
3 oz (75 g) currants
3 oz (75 g) caster sugar
1 large egg (lightly beaten)

METHOD

Sift the flour into a mixing bowl and rub in the butter or margarine until the mixture resembles breadcrumbs. Add the currants and the sugar. Beat the egg, and stir into the mixture. Use your hands to make a dough and add some milk if it is a little too dry.

Roll the dough out on a floured working surface, to about $\frac{1}{4}$ (5 mm) thick and cut it into rounds with a $2\frac{1}{2}$ (6.5 cm) cutter. (Makes about 20.)

Traditionally, a heavy griddle is used to cook Welsh cakes but a good solid frying pan will do. Heat the griddle over a medium heat and cook the cakes for about 2–3 minutes on each side. Make sure they are cooked through and have a good golden brown colour.

NEIL KINNOCK

Serve Welsh Cakes as they are, or buttered, with good Welsh honey.

PHILIP MADOC

Ginger Mousse

RECIPE

1 tbs (15 ml) powdered gelatine
5 tbs (75 ml) cold water
¾ pt (450 ml) evaporated milk
4 eggs (separated)
4 oz (100 g) caster sugar
pinch of salt
6 tbs (90 ml) rum
6 oz (175 g) crystallised ginger (finely chopped)

METHOD

Spoon the water into a small bowl. Sprinkle the gelatine over and leave to 'sponge' for 5 minutes. Beat the egg yolks with the sugar until they are very thick and pale yellow. Heat the milk to boiling and pour over the eggs. Return to the heat and cook gently, stirring constantly, until the custard is thick enough to coat the spoon. Remove from the heat and add the gelatine, whisking to dissolve. Leave until just cool, but not beginning to set. Beat the egg whites with salt until stiff. Add the rum and ginger to the custard, mixing well. Stir in a quarter of the egg whites, then fold in the rest gently. Pour into serving bowl and chill until set. *Serves 6.*

Mother-in-Law's Pavlova Cake

RECIPE

3 egg whites
6 oz (175 g) caster sugar
1 tsp (5 ml) vinegar
pinch of salt
few drops of vanilla essence

½ pt (300 ml) double cream (whipped)
8 oz (225 g) fresh fruit (eg strawberries)
1 tbs (15 ml) icing sugar
greaseproof paper

METHOD

Beat the egg whites until stiff. Add the sugar, vinegar, salt and vanilla essence and beat again until stiff. Wet one side of the greaseproof paper and lightly grease the other. Place the greaseproof paper on the baking sheet and pile the mixture on the greased side, forming a circle of about 8 in (20 cm) in diameter. Cook for 2 hours at Gas Mark 1 or 275°F/140°C. Turn off the heat, but leave the Pavlova in the oven until completely cold – this helps prevent cracking. Just before serving spread whipped cream on top of the Pavlova and arrange fresh fruit on top of the cream. Dust with icing sugar. *Serves 6.*

MAVIS
NICHOLSON

"This is a nice, easy recipe that is delicious in the summer with a sorbet, or just some biscuits."

Pears in Cassis

RECIPE

4 large pears (peeled)
1 oz (25 g) cornflour
4 fl oz (100 ml) Cassis liqueur
4 oz (100 g) fresh or frozen blackcurrants
mint leaves to decorate
2 pt (1.2 l) water
8 oz (225 g) caster sugar
cinnamon stick

METHOD

To make the syrup: put water, sugar and cinnamon in a saucepan and bring to the boil. Place the pears in the syrup, cover and poach for 15–20 minutes or until they are tender. Mix the cornflour with 3 tbs (45 ml) syrup. Add rest of syrup and cassis liqueur. Bring to the boil and simmer for 1 minute until thick. Leave to cool. Divide half the sauce and blackcurrants between 4 dishes. Place the pears on top and cover them with the rest of the sauce. Decorate with mint leaves.
Serves 4.

QUEEN MOTHER'S CAKE

The Famous Recipe for The Queen Mother's Favourite Cake

RECIPE

For the cake
8 oz (225 g) chopped dates
6 fl oz (175 ml) boiling water
1 tsp (5 ml) bicarbonate of soda
8 oz (225 g) caster sugar
8 oz (225 g) butter (softened)
1 egg (beaten)
10 oz (275 g) plain flour (sifted)
1 tsp (5 ml) baking powder

2 oz (50 g) walnuts (chopped)
1 tsp (5 ml) vanilla essence
For the topping
5 tbs (75 ml) soft brown sugar
2 tbs (30 ml) butter
2 tbs (30 ml) double cream
2 oz (50 g) walnuts (chopped)
9 × 12 (23 × 30 cm) tin (base-lined and greased)

METHOD

Place the dates in a bowl and pour over the boiling water. Stir in the bicarbonate of soda. Leave to stand for at least 30 minutes. Mix together the sugar, butter, egg, flour, baking powder, walnuts and vanilla essence in a large mixing bowl, then beat for 2–3 minutes until light and fluffy. Stir in the date mixture, then spoon into the prepared tin. Bake for 35–40 minutes at Gas Mark 4 or 350°F/180°C.

Leave to cool in the tin for 10 minutes before turning out. Place all other ingredients, except nuts, in a heavy-based saucepan. Slowly bring to the boil, stirring until the sugar has dissolved. Boil for 3 minutes; the mixture should have a fudge-like consistency – do not overcook or it will turn to toffee.

Spread the topping on the cake and sprinkle with the nuts.

STEVE RACE

"My cheesecake recipe is ideal for someone who, like myself, would rather eat than do anything else in the world (except drink), preferably while listening to Mozart and in the company of a beautiful woman. For the fullest appreciation, the cook should open a bottle of 1927 *Chateau Fabuleux*, drink half before starting and the other half before retiring – perhaps permanently!"

Cheesecake

RECIPE

6 oz (175 g) shortcrust pastry, or
4 trifle sponges
3 eggs
7 oz (200 g) caster sugar
1½ lb (675 g) curd cheese
2 oz (50 g) flour

¼ pt (150 ml) double cream
pinch of salt
grated rind and juice of 1 large lemon
8 in (20 cm) loose-bottomed cake tin (greased and floured)

METHOD

Line the tin with shortcrust pastry, or crumble the sponges and sprinkle over the base and press down well. Whisk the eggs and sugar until pale and thick. Beat the cheese with a wooden spoon, then add flour and beat thoroughly. Stir in the cream, salt, lemon rind and juice. Combine the two mixtures, again beating well. Pour the mixture into prepared tin and bake at Gas Mark 4 or 350°F/180°C for $1\frac{1}{4}$ hours. Turn off the oven and open the door slightly, but leave cake for $\frac{1}{4}$ hour before removing, so that it does not relax too quickly. It is best to wait overnight before cutting. *Serves 6.*

Bread & Butter Pudding

BRIAN
REDHEAD

RECIPE

3 slices bread and butter
1 oz (25 g) sultanas
1 oz (25 g) currants
1 oz (25 g) granulated sugar
For the custard

1 egg
1 egg yolk
1 tbs (15 ml) granulated sugar
½ pt (300 ml) milk
2 tbs (30 ml) brandy

METHOD

Butter a pie dish and cut the bread and butter into four pieces each. Put a layer of bread and butter in the bottom of a pie dish. Sprinkle the sultanas, currants and sugar over the bread and butter. Repeat this, finishing with a layer of bread with the butter side up.

To make the custard lightly beat the egg and yolk. Put the sugar, milk and brandy in a pan, slowly bring to boil and pour on to the beaten eggs, stirring all the time. Strain custard over the bread and butter. Sprinkle with sugar. Place dish in a bain-marie and cook at Gas Mark 4 or 350°F/180°C for 30–40 minutes, or until the custard is set and the top well-rounded and crusty. Serve hot in the dish. *Serves 4.*

137

ROBERT ROBINSON

Whisky Bananas

RECIPE

6 bananas (peeled)
3 tbs (45 ml) sugar (preferably demerara)
½ oz (10 g) butter
3 tbs (45 ml) whisky

METHOD

Heat the butter in a pan and fry the bananas. Sprinkle on the sugar. When the sugar has dissolved, remove from the heat and pour on the whisky. Serve at once with cream or yoghurt. *Serves 4.*

Bavaroise de la Rue

RECIPE

½ pt (300 ml) boiling milk
2 eggs (separated)
2 oz (50 g) caster sugar
½ oz (10 g) powdered gelatine
vanilla essence
strawberry essence

pink food colouring
¼ pt (150 ml) strawberry jelly (made at normal strength)
2 oz (50 g) sponge fingers (crumbled)
4–6 tbs (60–90 ml) Kirsch to taste
¼ pt (150 ml) double cream

METHOD

Cream the egg yolks with sugar until thick and creamy. Pour over the boiling milk, stirring continuously. Return to the pan on a low heat. Stir until the mixture thickens and coats the back of a spoon, but do not boil. Remove from the heat and sprinkle the gelatine over. Stir until dissolved and pass through a fine strainer. Divide into two equal parts in two clean bowls. Add two drops of vanilla essence to one half and two drops of strawberry essence to the other, with a little pink food colouring. Leave in a cool place, stirring occasionally until near setting point.

Pour the strawberry jelly into a 3 pt (1.8 l) mould and leave to set. Crumble sponge fingers and soak in Kirsch. Fold the lightly beaten cream and stiffly beaten egg-whites equally into the two bowls. Pour the vanilla mixture into the jelly mould. Sprinkle the crumbled sponge fingers over. Top with the strawberry mixture. Allow to set for 2 hours in the refrigerator. Then shake and turn on to a silver dish and pipe with whipped cream. Serves 4–6.

"Although this is one of my favourite sweets, I basically enjoy good, plain food – particularly casseroles, cooked long and slow."

DR ROBERT RUNCIE

Mulberry & Apple Summer Pudding

RECIPE

2¼ lb (1 kg) mulberries
2 cooking apples [approximately 1 lb (450 g)]
1 lb (450 g) sugar
¾ pt (450 ml) water
small loaf day-old white bread

METHOD

Wash the mulberries; peel, core and thinly slice the apples. Gently heat the sugar in the water until dissolved, then boil rapidly for 5 minutes. Add the fruit and simmer for about 10 minutes until pulpy. Press through a plastic or stainless-steel sieve.

Slice the bread thinly, cutting off the crusts. Use to cover the bottom of a soufflé dish. Spoon in enough of the purée to cover the bread completely. Add another layer of bread, and continue with alternate layers of bread and fruit purée until the dish is full. Place a small plate on the top, weighted down, and refrigerate overnight on a plate or tray to catch any juices.

Turn out the pudding and serve with whipped cream.

Scottish Shortbread

RECIPE

1 lb (450 g) plain flour
8 oz (225 g) caster sugar
8 oz (225 g) fine semolina
1 lb (450 g) butter

METHOD

Mix all dry ingredients together. Rub in the butter. Press into a shallow 10 × 14 in (25 × 36 cm) tin. Prick all over with a fork and bake at Gas Mark 2 or 300°F/150°C for about an hour. Mark into fingers while still warm and allow to cool in the tin. Store in an airtight container.

SELINA SCOTT

Traditional Scottish shortbread is made in one piece and cut into wedges or fingers after baking. Adding semolina gives the shortbread a crunchy texture.

141

BARRY **S**HEENE

"This is a recipe for a special apple tart. It's from a tiny village where we used to spend our holidays in Venezuela. It's about the most fattening thing you can eat and it tastes great."

Torta de la Casa

RECIPE

8 oz (225 g) butter
8 oz (225 g) caster sugar
3 eggs (lightly beaten)
1 lb (450 g) plain flour
1 tsp (5 ml) baking powder
3–4 tbs (45–60 ml) milk

1 lb (450 g) cooking apples (peeled, cored and thinly sliced)
2 oz (50 g) soft brown sugar
2 tsp (10 ml) ground cinnamon
8 × 10 in (20 × 25 cm) roasting tin (base-lined and greased)

METHOD

Cream together the butter and sugar until light and fluffy. Add the eggs, one at a time, beating after each addition. Sift together the flour and baking powder and fold in with enough milk to make a thick cake mixture.

Mix together the apple slices, brown sugar and cinnamon. Spoon a third of the cake mixture into the tin and top with half the apple slices. Repeat, then finish with a layer of cake mixture.

Bake towards the top of the oven at Gas Mark 4 or 350°F/180°C for 50 minutes – 1 hour, or until a skewer inserted into the cake comes out clean. Allow to cool in the tin.

Banana & Toffee Flan

(Bonaffi Pie)

RECIPE

9 oz (250 g) digestive biscuits (crushed)
3 oz (75 g) butter
2 × 14 oz (400 g) tins condensed milk
3 or 4 bananas (peeled)
½ pt (300 ml) double cream (whipped)

METHOD

Melt butter in saucepan. Add crushed biscuit and mix together thoroughly. Spoon into a 10 in (25 cm) flan dish and press down well. Put into fridge to set. Place unopened tins of condensed milk in a saucepan of water. Cover and boil for 2 hours keeping tins of milk submerged all the time. Remove tins from water using oven gloves and allow to cool for 10 minutes. The condensed milk will have caramelised into a rich golden colour, with a toffee flavour. Take biscuit base out of fridge. Slice bananas and arrange on top of base. Open tins of condensed milk and spread evenly over the bananas. Allow to cool and top with whipped cream. *Serves 6.*

Len Smith

President of Rotary International
in Great Britain and Ireland

DAVID STEEL

Athelbrose

RECIPE

2 oz (50 g) oatmeal
½ pt (300 ml) double cream
2 tbs (30 ml) honey
whisky to taste

METHOD

Toast the oatmeal under a grill. Whip the double cream until thick, then fold the oatmeal, honey and whisky into the cream. Fresh fruit, such as raspberries or loganberries, can also be added.

Summer Pudding

RECIPE

1 lb (450 g) raspberries
1 lb (450 g) strawberries (hulled)
½ lb (225 g) redcurrants (stalks removed)
½ lb (225 g) caster sugar (the mixture should end up sweet but tart)
10–15 slices of fresh wholemeal bread according to the size of the dish

METHOD

Heat fruit and sugar and simmer gently until sugar dissolves. Bring mixture slowly to the boil. Simmer for 2 minutes only (the fruit should be still intact but very juicy). Remove crusts from the bread and cut into triangles. Line a dish with pieces of bread, so that no spaces are left. Pour in fruit mixture. Cover with rest of bread. Place a small plate or saucer on top, then on top of that, put a 3 lb (1.4 kg) weight. Leave in the refrigerator overnight. Turn out of dish. Serve chilled with double cream.

MIRIAM STOPPARD

"A very old, traditional recipe of a pudding usually eaten by peasants because the ingredients were so easy and cheap to come by, now enjoying the dubious patronage of the university-educated housewife. It can be stored in the deep freeze for several months. We're still eating the puddings I made last summer!"

BARBARA THORN

Inspector Frazer from *The Bill*

Too-Too-Divine Chocolate Cake

RECIPE

8 oz (225 g) plain chocolate
8 oz (225 g) butter
2 eggs
8 oz (225 g) digestive biscuits
1 oz (25 g) glacé cherries (chopped)
2 tbs (30 ml) brandy or rum
extra glacé cherries to decorate

METHOD

Butter a 6-7 inch (15-18 cm) cake tin with a loose base. Break the chocolate into squares and place in a basin over a pan of simmering water. Remove basin as soon as the chocolate has melted. Place butter in another small pan and melt in the same way. Lightly beat the eggs and pour butter into eggs in a steady stream, stirring continuously. Add melted chocolate and beat well. Place biscuits in a paper or plastic bag and crush with a rolling pin. Stir into chocolate mixture with the cherries and rum or brandy. Spoon mixture into prepared tin. Decorate with cherries and leave to set in a fridge over night. Remove from the tin and serve, cut into wedges.

Chocolate Mousse

RECIPE

4 eggs (separated)
4 oz (100 g) plain chocolate
1 oz (25 g) softened butter
juice of one small orange or 1 tbs (15 ml) Grand Marnier or Cointreau

METHOD

Break chocolate into squares, put in a small mixing bowl and heat over a pan of water until the chocolate has melted. Allow to cool for a few minutes, then stir in the beaten egg yolks and mix. Add the softened butter and orange juice or liqueur and mix in well without beating.

Whisk the egg whites and fold into the chocolate mixture. Spoon into 4 glasses or little pots and refrigerate, for at least 1 hour before serving. *Serves 4.*

FRANCIS WILSON

Pêches Brûlée

RECIPE

6 fresh peaches (skinned)
2 tbs (30 ml) Cointreau
½ pt (300 ml) double cream (whipped)
4 oz (100 g) soft brown sugar

METHOD

Halve the peaches, remove the stones and place in a shallow dish. Pour the Cointreau over the peaches, then spread the cream over to cover them completely, and sprinkle with sugar. Place under preheated hot grill for about 3 minutes or until the sugar has caramelised. Allow to cool and chill before serving. *Serves 6.*

Red Wine Punch

RECIPE

1 75 cl bottle red wine
12 sugar lumps
6 whole cloves
1 cinnamon stick
1 pt (600 ml) boiling water
¼ pt (150 ml) Curaçao
¼ pt (150 ml) brandy
grated nutmeg

METHOD

Pour the wine into a saucepan, add sugar lumps, cloves and cinnamon stick. Heat gently until just below boiling point. Add boiling water, Curaçao and brandy. Pour into warmed glasses and sprinkle grated nutmeg on top. Serve at once.

JOHN HART
(COXSWAIN)
BARRY DOCK STATION,
WALES
RNLB 'ARUN'
(Arun class)

TONY BENN

Tea

Take 1 pint of pure water and boil it in a kettle with North Sea gas. Add one tea bag from the Commonwealth, some milk and sugar from the Third World and stir until the tea assumes a satisfying, deep brown colour.

Then remove the tea bag and take a cup every hour, or more often, if necessary.

Sheepish

RECIPE

8 oz (225 g) carton Greek sheep's milk yoghurt
2 oz (50 g) good quality bitter chocolate

METHOD

Chill the yoghurt. Freeze the chocolate for 30 minutes, then smash into small pieces. Stir into the yoghurt and serve immediately, while the chocolate is still hard. *Serves 1.*

RABBI LIONEL BLUE

"This is a simple recipe – odd, but I like it. It is quite sophisticated in a funny sort of way."

ROY
CASTLE

Stuffed Camel

RECIPE

72 hard boiled eggs — shelled and stuffed equally into:
24 fish, headed, tailed, finned and filleted and stuffed equally into:
6 chickens, headed, legged and plucked and stuffed equally into:
1 sheep, sheared, headed and legged and stuffed equally into:
1 camel.

METHOD

No basting necessary if Camel has just visited a water hole. Cook at Gas Mark 3 or 325°F/160°C for 9 days or until tender.
This is a genuine dish eaten at Bedouin weddings. In order to sample such a feast one must either marry a Bedouin or get invited to a "Bedouin Weddouing".

Fish Buttie

Take four freshly fried fish fingers and put between two slices of white bread, with butter, salt and lashings of vinegar. Wash down with plenty of hot, sweet tea.

MICHAEL ELPHICK

★ MICHAEL ★
ELPHICK

Michael is a keen fisherman, and on those rare occasions when he can take a break from work, he likes nothing better than to get away on a fishing trip.

GARFIELD

Chicken Casserole à la Garfield

Find a live, fat, feathery, slow chicken —

Corner . . .

POUNCE!

MICHAEL
GRADE

Bloody Mary

RECIPE

2 fl oz (50 ml) vodka
2 fl oz (50 ml) tomato juice
1 tsp (5 ml) Worcestershire sauce
1 tsp (5 ml) Angostura bitters
1 tsp (5 ml) lemon juice
salt and pepper

METHOD

Mix the ingredients in a glass jug and chill well before serving.

Michael likes to add a little French mustard, creamed horseradish, grapefruit and lemon juice and serves a stick of celery and pickled onion with *his* Bloody Mary!

155

Mayonnaise

Talking about my latest novel *Medusa* set on the island of Menorca, at a literary convention, I told the story of Cardinal Richelieu's chef faced with an abundance of *oleo* and *huevo* and not much else with which to make a sauce. A little experimentation and he settled for a whipped-up mix of egg-yolks and olive oil, and since the bone of contention between the British and the French was Mahon, the finest port in the Western Mediterranean, and as the Cardinal's residence was in Mahon he called it. ... yes, you've guessed it – Mahonnaise.

Granny Michelmore's Rhubarb Chutney

RECIPE

2 lb (900 g) rhubarb [cut into 1 inch (2·5 cm) chunks]
juice 2 lemons
1 pt (600 ml) vinegar
1 oz (25 g) ginger root

1 clove garlic
2 lb (900 g) demerara sugar
½ tsp (2·5 ml) cayenne pepper
1 lb (450 g) sultanas
1 oz (25 g) salt

METHOD

Put rhubarb, lemon juice and vinegar into a large pan. Bruise the ginger and place in a muslin bag; cut garlic into small pieces, and add to the rhubarb. Boil until fruit is tender and the volume of the fruit has been reduced to two-thirds, stirring occasionally. Add the sugar, cayenne, garlic, sultanas and salt. Stir over a gentle heat until the sugar has dissolved. Bring to the boil and boil rapidly, stirring occasionally, for about 10–12 minutes, then test for setting. When set, allow the chutney to cool in the pan for 10 minutes. Remove ginger. Pour into clean warm jars, and cover. Store in a cool dry place. Keep for at least one month before using. Makes 3½–4 lbs (1·6–1·8 kg).

CLIFF MICHELMORE

ROLAND
RAT

"Great stuff, Rat Fans!"

Rat Cocktail

RECIPE

3 fresh strawberries
3 scoops of pink ice cream
1 banana
½ pt (300 ml) milk
fresh cream for topping
chocolate bits for garnishing

METHOD

Find a glass or a bucket! (preferably pink)
Be prepared to throw everthin in!
chop up the fruit
throw in the ice cream
sling in the milk
mix vigerusly
slop the cream on top
throw on your choki bits
get a straw
sluff it thro it! Loverly Yeahh!

Instant Pick-Me-Up

For hard-working people – and Lifeboatmen:

RECIPE

3 eggs (beaten)
5 tbs (75 ml) Horlicks
2 tbs (30 ml) drinking chocolate powder
1 pt (600 ml) milk
3 scoops vanilla or chocolate ice cream

METHOD

Blend, whisk or stir thoroughly all the above ingredients and drink at your own risk. *Serves 1.*

"This, taken throughout the day instead of meals, will give you plenty of energy output (and eventually cardiac arrest). Seriously, I do use this instead of a meal when I am working hard and find that it really does work."

ACKNOWLEDGEMENTS

The Automobile Association and the Royal National Lifeboat Institution wish to thank the following for contributing recipes which we were unable to use and, in some cases, cash donations to the funds of the RNLI:

Natalie Anglesey, Michael Aspel, Adam Athanassiou, Bill Beaumont, Michael Blakey, Barbara Taylor Bradford, Faith Brown, Douglas Cameron, Robin Cousins, Steve Cram, Gemma Craven, Timothy Dalton, Jim Davidson, Barbara Dickson, Janet Ellis, Kaffe Fassett, Dawn French, Lady Hart of South Lanark, Nigel Havers, Thora Hird, Gordon Honeycombe, Sally James, Caron Keating, Bonnie Langford, Lulu, Alfred Lynch, Magnus Magnusson, Geraldine McEwan, John Motson, Terry Nutkins, Derek Redmond, Anneka Rice, Jim Rosenthal, Pam Royle, Peter Sallis, Jimmy Savile, Sir Harry Secombe, David Smith, Alvin Stardust, Steve Thompson, Roger Whittaker, Trish Williamson, Ernie Wise.

Special thanks are due to the following for the use of their photographs, for which acknowledgements were requested:

Mike Evans, Philips Classics Productions (Sir Colin Davis); William F Flett (Coxswain Peter Murray); Thames Television (Barbara Thorn – *The Bill*); United Feature Syndicate (Garfield); A J Young, (Atlantic 21 lifeboat).